Beyond Certainty

Beyond Certainty

A Phenomenological Approach to Moral Reflection

Don E. Marietta Jr.

LEXINGTON BOOKS
Lanham • Boulder • New York • Toronto • Oxford

LEXINGTON BOOKS

Published in the United States of America
by Lexington Books
An imprint of The Rowman & Littlefield Publishing Group, Inc.
4501 Forbes Boulevard, Suite 200, Lanham, Maryland 20706

PO Box 317
Oxford
OX2 9RU, UK

British Library Cataloguing in Publication Information Available

Library of Congress Cataloging-in-Publication Data

Marietta, Don E. Jr.
  Beyond certainty : A phenomenological approach to moral reflection / Don E.
Marietta Jr.
     p. cm.
  Includes bibliographical references and index.
  ISBN 0-7391-0732-1 (cloth : alk. paper)
  1. Ethics. I. Title.
BJ1012.M362 2004
170'.22   2003066134

Printed in the United States of America

∞™ The paper used in this publication meets the minimum requirements of American
National Standard for Information Sciences—Permanence of Paper for Printed Library
Materials, ANSI/NISO Z39.48-1992.

Contents

Introduction

The relationship between knowledge and moral obligation is one of the most important issues in ethical theory. It is also one of the most difficult and complex. A simple yes or no is not adequate to answer the question of whether moral rightness and wrongness are related to what the agent knows. There are a variety of explanations of why moral judgments are independent of knowledge, and there are even more ways to explain that there is a close connection between correct moral judgment and knowledge. Since I believe that there is a connection between knowledge and obligation, my greatest interest is in the latter explanations. It is important to me to separate my position from claims that I do not think are supportable.

In the chapters that follow, it will be necessary to deal with theories that deny a close connection between knowledge and morality. I will not give much space to explaining my rejection of the kind of moral relativism that is based on cultural relativism and sees moral right and wrong as judgments made by a society just for that society. Reasons for rejecting this kind of relativism are amply presented in ethics textbooks. I reject theories that deny that moral judgments are knowledge claims about the actions that are judged, but only reveal something about the persons making the judgments. Emotivism and prescriptivism have been thoroughly explored, and there is no need for me to repeat the arguments against these subjectivist theories. I rejected subjectivist theories for the widely accepted reasons that are explained in the literature.

Of greater concern to me are concepts of moral knowledge that claim too much. I will not defend any belief that we have infallible, or even indubitable, knowledge of moral right and wrong. Claims that moral knowledge is innate, or that we have the ability to intuit it, I believe to be not only mistaken, but actually detrimental to the moral enterprise. Such perfect knowledge is not necessary in morality, any more than it is necessary, or even possible, in other aspects of life.

I do not think approaches that would base moral judgment on deductions from moral knowledge, sometimes called foundationalism, can be supported. The relationship between what we know about the world and human beings and our sense of moral obligation is much more subtle than many moral philosophers have acknowledged. I do not believe that we can develop adequate moral judgments without knowledge, but to describe the relationship I see between knowledge and a sense of moral obligation, I must explore the phenomenology of moral thinking and decision making and explain several "tools" to be used in making judgments.

First I will show that there is no dichotomy between factual judgments and moral or value judgments as we first become aware of the elements of knowing and evaluating as we reflect on the world as we experience it. In concrete reflection of our primal experiences of the world, that is, experiences that have not been shaped by the categories and schemes within which we learn to catalog our experiences, we discover that the matters that can be constituted as facts and as values are together, not distinguished and separated. An explanatory scheme in which values are derived from facts and depend upon them has not yet shaped our way of seeing the basic elements of experience.

The concept of "primal experience" grows out of phenomenological writing about the Lifeworld, sometimes called the lived world. Edmund Husserl's work, which began with an emphasis on the philosophy of mathematics and logic, came to include analysis of human experience of the world (the Lifeworld). His latter works, especially, speak of the Lifeworld, which he described as the perspective, or "horizon," of human consciousness of the world. I am not attempting a full explanation of the concept of a Lifeworld, and I am certainly not claiming to exposit the view of the Lifeworld held by Husserl or by any other phenomenologist. I am simply acknowledging that concepts of a Lifeworld are the background from which my ideas developed. I was also influenced by Jean-Paul Sartre's idea of pre-thetic knowledge, a concept he used in discussing the ontology of the self and the world it knows and in clarifying temporality. My view of our most primal awareness should not be taken as an exposition of Sartre's ideas.[1]

Fact and value and knowledge and moral sense are separated when we constitute them as separate and distinct notions and try to reunite them by means of deductive reasoning, reasoning that cannot avoid an impasse between "is" and "ought." Before this, they have come to us as related aspects of our primal experience. Since the connection that we see in our "untutored" awareness between the factual and valuational aspects might be correct or might be mistaken in regard to a particular aspect of the world with which we are engaged, our lived worlds, we need to use some means of assessing the values and moral feelings that come in our primitive reflection. I call these tools of judgment. One tool is finding intersubjective support of our valuational as well as factual judgments. Another tool is discovering fittingness in terms of compatibility with what we know about ourselves and the world and the values by which we have lived satisfactorily. Another tool is examining the adequacy of our personal worldview in terms of its contents and the way we have come to hold it. The use of these tools requires careful reflection, and it is important that we employ the right kind of reflection.

Some types of reflection preclude sensitive and creative making of judgments, since they restrict us to thinking too abstractly and using reductionistic methods. This is a result of reflection on abstract notions, broad categories, and highly theoretical formulations. When philosophers have engaged in what they considered reflection, they have tended to think on a highly theoretical level. I advocate reflection that keeps us closely in touch with the actual things and events of life and does not force our thoughts and feelings into intellectual Procrustean beds. This is concrete reflection that is directed toward the matters of experience as we engage the world.

The reflection that best leads us to correct moral judgments is not easy. It is not mysterious or cultish or a "new age" fad. It must be rigorous, but its rigor does not lie in adherence to standards that have been developed in service to some of the special sciences. Its rigor does not lie in a commitment to naturalism. Rigor must come from reflection that can be shared with others, explained and subjected to critical review, and found to open up to us the richness of our engagement with the world.

Emphasis on remaining close to our lived worlds almost forces a contextual approach to moral judgment. In chapter 4, I deal with some of the advantages of contextualism and its connection with concrete reflection. In chapter 5, I argue for a pluralistic approach that takes advantage of several basic sources of value. Contextualism and pluralism must be used responsibly. They cannot be used as excuses for arbitrariness or self-serving decisions. The chapters on these approaches examine the methods by which irresponsible judgments can be avoided.

Chapter 6 deals with the role that moral philosophy has played in giving the impression that ethics has been a mere battleground of conflicting opinions and has made no progress in resolving ethical dilemmas. The concluding chapter deals with the adequacy of the system I outline. I do not want to make unwarranted claims for the approach, but I do argue that it is adequate to enable well-intentioned people who are willing to do the work to make good moral judgments in most situations. Even though there might be some cases in which there is no way to use sound knowledge in the service of sound moral judgment, these will be rare. In almost all cases, responsible thinkers will be able to do as well in making moral judgments as they can do in other areas of life, such as making decisions about health, use of money, and interpersonal relationships. This is not all that moral philosophers have wanted from ethical theory, but I believe it is all we can reasonably expect, and it is all we need.

NOTES

1. For a general introduction to phenomenology, as well as an explanation of the concept of the "lived world," see David Stewart and Algis Mickunas, *Exploring Phenomenology* (Chicago: American Library Association, 1974) [Check index for various concepts of the "lived world" concept.]; see Jean-Paul Sartre, *Being and Nothingness*, trans. Hazel E. Barnes (New York:Washington Square Press [Pocket Books], 1966: esp. 13, 26, and 211; for recent treatment of the work of Edmund Husserl, see entry by Philip Buckley in *Encyclopedia of Phenomenology*, ed. Lester Embree; et al. (Dordrecht: Kluwer Academic Publishers, 1997), 326–33. *See also* entry by Don Welton on "World" in *Encyclopedia of Phenomenology*, 736–43.

Chapter One

The Possibility of Moral Knowledge

Can there be any moral knowledge? Would it be limited to a priori knowledge? Can knowledge of the world contribute to knowledge of right and wrong behavior? Answering these questions takes us beyond normative ethics to metaethics, the exploration of various aspects of the logic of ethics. Examining the meaning of terms used in moral discourse was one of the first aspects of metaethics to be developed. From the meaning of words, metaethics progresses to analysis of moral experience, especially that of making moral judgments. Finally, metaethics must deal with the justification of ethical principles and moral judgments.

METAETHICS

From the beginnings of ethical theory in Greek philosophy, thinkers have paid attention to the meaning of the terms used in moral discourse. Plato was concerned with the meaning of such concepts as justice, goodness, and happiness, and he used his metaphysical doctrines to justify his interpretation of these concepts and the important place he gave them in his ethical doctrines. Plato's effort to define moral terms might be the beginning of metaethics. The term "metaethics" suggests going above or beyond ethics, but it is really something that goes before or underlies careful ethical thinking. It prepares the way for normative ethics, for the development of ethical theory and for the making of moral decisions and judgments. It might be understood as a study of the logic of ethics in a broad sense.

Metaethics as preparation for normative ethics precedes building of theory, such as explaining and defending Utilitarianism, Kantian ethics of duty, or feminist ethics. There have been claims that metaethics is neutral in regard to normative ethical theories, and this seems to be true to a great extent. Metaethics does not support any theory directly, but could reveal logical weaknesses in the presentation of a theory.

Defining terms used in ethical discourse is one aspect of metaethics, and the importance of this is not hard to see. Metaethics goes beyond defining terms, however, to examining the nature of moral judgments. When a person says that stealing is wrong, what is being done? Is the person making a factual statement about stealing? Perhaps that is what is intended, but the intention would rest on confusion if there is no moral knowledge or any identifiable moral qualities that the statement can denote. Is a moral judgment no more than an expression of feeling? There have been a number of theories about this and many arguments over the matter. Down through the centuries most moral philosophers have assumed that people were reporting something they knew about an activity when they said it is right or wrong.

In this century especially, the view that moral claims are knowledge claims was called into question. Some philosophers supported a view called emotivism, which held that moral judgments were actually expression, or even just ventilation, of positive or negative feelings toward some behavior. Others, called imperativists or prescriptivists, held that moral judgments are thinly veiled attempts to influence the behavior of other people. If these interpretations are correct, a moral judgment is not really a statement that can tell us something about the behavior in question. Stating a moral judgment is itself a behavior that reveals something about the one speaking, not about the speaker's claim.[1]

Not all moral philosophers were willing to give up the idea that a moral judgment intends to say something about the behavior judged, and in fact does say something about the action being judged, and they have presented several metaethical approaches supporting a cognitivist position, an explanation of moral judgment as expression of knowledge or belief about the behavior judged.

The position I take on this issue is that moral judgments can rest on moral knowledge or, at least, moral judgment needs the support of knowledge, but we must deal with other matters before we get to that discussion.

We must deal with another facet of metaethics, the justification of moral beliefs. This is important, of course, if one is to hold that moral judgments can be more than expressions of sentiment, but it is the most difficult aspect of metaethics. Since most moral philosophers have not been willing to treat moral judgment as a matter of mere taste or preference, they have looked for reasons that support moral judgments, some basis on which some judgments can be shown to be correct and others to be mistaken. This difficult work has been an ongoing enterprise of moral philosophers. Some of them tried to support moral principles with metaphysics. Others appealed to widely held values or claimed that human nature or the needs of society demanded certain moral rules. Others have explained that there are rational processes for making decisions, and these can be used in making moral decisions as well as others.

In different ways philosophers tried to show a close connection between factual knowledge and moral obligation. The most ambitious approaches have claimed that factual knowledge, of the world or of human nature or of God, entailed specific moral obligations. A general designation for moral theories of this sort is ethical naturalism. Ethical naturalism came under severe attack because of logical problems that we will examine later. In attempts to hold onto a significant connection between factual knowledge and moral obligation, other approaches to ethics attempted to show that factual knowledge contributes to moral judgments, but with a connection looser than logical entailment.

As any form of ethical naturalism became difficult to support, a number of philosophers turned to ethical systems that did not face the logical problems that confront ethical naturalism, but still considered moral beliefs a form of knowledge. Claims that certain properties are good or bad, or that certain actions are right or wrong, were interpreted as knowledge about the actions or qualities in question, but the knowledge was not derived from knowledge of the world but was intuited, received directly as immediate knowledge. Several types of intuitionism were employed, but intuitionist approaches run into problems no less serious than those facing naturalism.[2]

As we seek a foundation for ethics in factual knowledge, we must proceed with caution. Any connection between knowledge and moral obligation must be understood with more logical subtlety and philosophical sophistication than approaches used in previous centuries or earlier in this century.

It seems obvious to people who are not conversant with metaethics that moral beliefs should be based on factual knowledge, the more knowledge the better. The claim that there is a logical impasse between knowledge and moral obligation probably seems unreasonable and perverse to them. Why would knowledge not at least throw some light on the principles on which good behavior should be based? What is this logical problem that keeps us from finding the foundation of our morality in what we know?

THE "IS/OUGHT" IMPASSE

The logical complication, which keeps factual knowledge from being the justification of moral judgments, was pointed out by David Hume in the eighteenth century. Hume saw that it is not logically valid to deduce statements of moral obligation, "ought" statements, from factual premises, "is" statements. In a valid deductive argument, nothing can be in the conclusion that is not entailed by the premises. One cannot argue that roses are red, and violets are blue, therefore hot soup helps cure a cold. There is nothing in the premises about either soups or colds and nothing about healing. This should be obvious to anyone. What is not as obvious, and what was largely ignored even after Hume explained it, is that it is just as invalid to base a moral obligation on purely factual premises. Unless one of the premises says something about moral obligation, the conclusion cannot be about moral obligation.

What Hume recognized is described as a dichotomy between factual knowledge and moral obligation and is called the "is/ought" impasse. A related problem is a dichotomy between factual knowledge and judgments of value, the fact/value dichotomy. These are somewhat different but closely related problems, and both of them seem at first sight to prevent the basing of ethical norms on factual information. The relationship between these two logical impasses is not simple because the relationship between valuing and making moral judgments is variously interpreted. They are related, however. They are the same kind of logical problem, and both are important aspects of making moral decisions. The fact/value and "is/ought" impasses are also related because positivistic analytical philosophical approaches to ethics have seen them as preventing the basing of moral judgments on any sort of factual information.

It is logically proper to acknowledge that normative claims, moral or aesthetic, cannot be deduced from purely factual premises. In the twentieth century many philosophers have taken seriously Hume's logical analysis of deductive moral arguments. Some philosophers, however, have gone further to conclude that there can be no connection at all between knowledge and obligation, except for the limited role of reason in ethics that Hume recognized. Hume held that through reason and observation we can discover the consequences of acting in certain ways, and we can come to realize what we esteem and what we despise. We will most likely act to secure what we esteem and avoid what we dislike, but the basic value judgments on which we act, he held, do not come from reasoning, for they are sentiments.[3]

Since G. E. Moore used the term "naturalistic fallacy" for ethical theories that defined moral words, such as "good," in terms of naturalistic factors such as being pleasurable or being the object of a person's desire, it has been almost a dogma for some philosophers that no form of ethical naturalism is acceptable. Moore's concept of a "naturalistic" fallacy has been seen by William Frankena and others to be somewhat confused. The correctness of his antinaturalistic stance is assumed in the concept of a "naturalistic" fallacy. The real problem that Moore saw was a problem of definitions, a problem that would apply to certain ways of explaining moral judgments naturalistically. The problem, however, is the familiar definist fallacy, the fallacy of confusing categories and defining a thing as something it is not. Moore was right in recognizing that some possible definitions of "good" would commit the definist fallacy, but he was tendentious in holding that any possible naturalistic moral judgment is fallacious. He did not show that naturalism is of itself fallacious. Only certain naturalistic arguments run afoul of the kind of logical error Moore had in mind.[4]

Kenneth R. Pahel doubts that there have been any ethical naturalists who actually held that moral obligations can be deduced from factual premises or held that moral principles can be "true by definition." He says it is a myth that some philosophers were obtuse enough to think this kind of naturalism possible. He explains that the ethical naturalists were doing something entirely different.[5]

I also have difficulty believing that ethical naturalists did not recognize the logical difference between factual descriptions and moral claims, but the myth that they made such ground-level mistakes is widely held, and the fear of ethical naturalism is so great that many philosophers carefully avoid any attempt to relate moral principles to factual knowledge.

I believe we can make effective use of factual knowledge in establishing basic moral principles, but the logic of doing this must be approached with care. It will require some new approaches to metaethics. The main burden of this book will be the explanation of an approach to ethics that employs new metaethical methods. The new approach will not be an attempt to show that the "is/ought" impasse is a mistaken logical principle. It is correct and important within the context of deductive logic. My approach will not be a matter of simply denying what Hume said, as I do not believe it is deniable. The new approach will require explaining the relationship between knowledge and obligation and the way moral judgments can be made in ways that do not run afoul of the logical impasses.

First let us see how the "is/ought" impasse affects moral thinking. A well-established pattern of logical reasoning avoids the "is/ought" impasse by using a moral principle as one premise in the moral argument. The pattern is like this:

Premise 1: A moral principle which is already accepted.
Premise 2: An observation about the action in question.
Conclusion: A judgment about what should be done.

An example of this pattern would be (1) it is wrong to cause harm to a person that does not benefit the person; (2) stealing harms a person and does not benefit the person; therefore, it is wrong to steal. The first premise states a general moral principle, and the second premise states the fact about stealing that it inflicts gratuitous injury. This fact about stealing makes it subject to moral disapproval on the basis of the moral principle already stated. Together the two premises justify the claim that stealing is wrong. This is a valid logical argument. Few people ever reason things out this formally, but there is no logical problem in doing so.

It is probably more common for someone to argue as follows: If you do not visit your mother during the holidays, you will hurt her feelings. You should visit her. Practically, there is no real problem here because the moral premise, it is wrong to hurt your mother, is assumed. In the statement of the argument it is repressed, usually because it is taken for granted by both people talking. The argument would fall apart, however, if a willful daughter asked, "Why should I be concerned about how she feels? She didn't hesitate to hurt my feelings when I said I was going to marry Peter." For the discussion to continue, it would be necessary to defend the principle that even mothers who have hurt their children by being judgmental should be treated with kindness and respect. It is necessary to know the logical form of the argument, even when it is presented in an abbreviated form.

It might be a good practice to take note of the absence of moral premises, because in other arguments the moral premise can be repressed in expectation that it will slip by without examination. The aggressive funeral director might put the following argument to the grieving daughter: Your mother's friends, Agnes and Martha, were buried in our eight-thousand-dollar silver alloy caskets. You should get the same quality casket for your mother. The distraught daughter might agree to this, never really asking why she should bury her mother in the same price casket used by people of her acquaintance, but of a far wealthier economic class.

Carefully stating the premise that has been suppressed can be a good exercise in moral thinking. Support for euthanasia using the statement, "They shoot horses, don't they" does not state the moral principle to which the argument appeals. These principles are worth examining. We would hardly accept the principle that people must be treated the same way horses are treated. The principle that we should show people the same mercy we show to horses is worth consideration. The argument—we should show people as much mercy as we show horses; horses are shot to relieve them of pain; therefore, hopelessly ill people should not be allowed to suffer for a long time—is logically valid. Whether it adequately supports a demand for euthanasia must be considered more carefully. There might be differences between humans and horses that would make the valid argument inadequate.

A valid argument might not be a sound argument. That is, one of the premises might not be true. We have various ways of determining whether the premises in an argument are true when only factual premises and a factual conclusion are involved. In a moral argument, how can we determine that the moral premise is true? We might show that it is widely accepted, but that is not enough to show that it is true. Can we show that it is a premise that should be accepted? This is where we confront the "is/ought" impasse. In order to show that our moral argument is sound, we need to demonstrate that our general moral principle is true, but if we cannot deduce our general principles from factual premises, what can we do?

Hume did not see this as a significant problem. He believed that people naturally have benevolent feelings toward other people that will make them want to do what will benefit the people affected by their actions. Adam Smith shared this belief, which was the basis of his expectation that people seeking their own welfare would bring about good for all. This optimism about human nature is not shared by all philosophers, and even Hume had to recognize that people do not act benevolently when they are hard-pressed in competition for scarce resources. In any case, is the way people feel an adequate basis for primary moral principles?

We are not often bothered by the "is/ought" impasse because we have a wealth of moral principles that we learned at home or which are supported by our religious organizations. Some of these moral principles have been taken for granted for generations. We may be quite secure in our moral principles when no one is asking us to justify them. What happens, however, when the moral terrain gets rough and is no longer familiar? What happens when other good people do not agree with our principles? We happen to be in a time when old trusted "truths" are called into question. Environmental issues now confront us for the first time. What is the proper role of humans in the system of nature? What are our rights and obligations? What are the proper uses to make of medical procedures unknown to us until recently? Should "miraculous" medical procedures be used to make dying last for weeks or months? Should they be used on infants who can never have a full life, even if they escape death in the nursery? Who should receive scarce medical resources? When advanced diagnostic tests show that a person is predisposed to a serious ailment, should the person be told even if nothing can be done to prevent the illness? Should insurance companies have access to information about a person's predisposition? What are our moral obligations toward the people who are made permanently unemployable by advanced manufacturing methods and new patterns of trade?

The large issues might seem overwhelming, and we might feel unable to understand them, much less make judgments about them. We might think that we can leave these things to politicians and government officials. Only on Election Day need we act on them. Even if we act this irresponsibly, we cannot escape from moral decision making. The more immediate everyday things still confront us. Parent and adult child disagree over premarital sex. Couples must decide about birth control even if their church teaches that it is wrong. When a young daughter becomes pregnant, abortion is an option. Even if the law allows refraining from heroic measures to keep Grandfather from dying, is it the morally right thing to do? What should we do about those things that are left up to us as individual persons?

We would look to people who know more than we do for guidance. Our physicians, our teachers, our scientists must surely know what we should do! But how can they? The "is/ought" impasse shows those who understand the logic of moral judgment that knowledge does not do what we want it to do.

Can we hope to face the new and confusing moral questions with some degree of reason? Can the information explosion help us at all? Many moral philosophers have come to the conclusion that we must decide which moral principles appeal to us and act according to them. This would be what the emotivist schools of ethics would tell us. Subjectivist approaches to ethics see moral principles as like those matters of taste about which there should be no disputing. Of course, it might be pointed out that some approaches to morals result in social unrest or behaviors that we would find distasteful, but this only pushes the matter back a step or two. Social unrest is fervently desired by people of some political persuasions. What some people consider ugly or distasteful behavior is seen by other people as beautiful expressions of freedom and people finding themselves. The right order in the eyes of the privileged is seen as a great wrong by those not favored by the social order.

BEYOND THE "IS/OUGHT" IMPASSE

How is rational ethics possible in the face of the "is/ought" impasse? We must see how older metaethical theories led many moral philosophers to rule out any form of ethical naturalism, any attempt to base ethics on factual description of the world.

A commonly accepted metaethical approach is based on concepts of justification that would make it impossible, in light of the "is/ought" impasse, to base moral principles on factual knowledge. This approach assumes that deductive argument, with a normative major premise, is the paradigm case of moral reasoning and that the "is/ought" impasse prevents basing normative judgments on factual premises. A logical barrier is raised between knowledge and obligation. In this situation, it is not surprising that emotivism or prescriptivism seemed the only acceptable approaches. With these ethical theories, there is no need to provide a logical justification for basic moral principles. With these approaches, basic moral principles are adopted. The best justification for adopting one set of principles over another is that the set of principles leads to a more attractive way of life, a better society. The judgment that the way of life is attractive or the society a good one is itself a matter of opinion. Since the adopted principles provide the general premises in moral arguments, and the choice of principles is itself a moral decision, can we escape the subjectivism of believing that morality is just a matter of personal opinion, with no right or wrong, only likes and dislikes? Such a moral subjectivism is only a step away from moral skepticism.

Many of us do not want to fall into moral skepticism. Is there anything we can do to avoid it? Can we show that the notion of a gap between factual information and duty has been mistakenly interpreted? I believe we can show that the "is/ought" impasse does not preclude all connection between knowledge and moral obligation. It does rule out some metaethical approaches, but not all.

We need to examine more carefully the logical impasse. It is a restriction on making certain moves in a logical argument; the problem lies in the logical relationship between statements used in a deductive argument. It has not been shown that the "is/ought" impasse applies directly to moral insights and moral judgments as such if these are not derived by deductive argument. I believe the "is/ought" impasse applies only when deductive argument is used in moral reasoning. The importance that many philosophers have given to deductive argument is the problem I see with traditional metaethics. The deductive argumentation that these philosophers have seen as the paradigm of moral thought is not needed in moral reasoning, and it is seldom used when people make serious moral decisions. Seldom do people arrive at their moral judgments by deductive arguments.

The traditional pattern of moral argument is an ideal type that appears in ethics textbooks more often than it is used in actual decisions about behavior. The "is/ought" impasse certainly shows us that we cannot use formal deductive logic to establish our most general moral principles. These basic principles are the sources of such normative premises as are used in valid deductive arguments of the textbook sort. There are no principles from which the most general principles could be derived. If deductive reasoning were the only acceptable way to deal with moral thought, our most general principles would be arbitrary, and we would simply adopt them even though they have no rational basis. Some philosophers have believed that this is what we do, merely adopt basic principles because they somehow appeal to us. I do not believe this is the case.

To understand that there are rational grounds for adopting basic moral principles, we must be willing to go beyond formal deductive logic. We need not have a great sense of loss when we give up the idea of depending on deductive logic to do a job it cannot do. We have never been so enamored of deductive logic as to use it regularly in our decision making, and we do not always trust the deductions of people who would convince us of something. Have we not had the experience of being confronted with a deductive argument claiming that we should do something, not do something, or accept some behavior as right, only to feel uncertain about the claim presented? The argument might be valid, and the premises seem to be true, and still it did not bring conviction. We have been more assured in using deductive argument to refute claims than in using it to prove them. Now the "is/ought" impasse shows us that we cannot use deductive arguments to validate our basic moral principles.

Where do we turn? The way I propose calls upon us to enter modes of thought with which many philosophers are not comfortable. We must deal with the interface between the logical thinking with which philosophers have long been familiar and the phenomenology of thinking about moral concerns. This will appear to some philosophers to be a confusion of philosophy and psychology. It is not; phenomenology is not empirical psychology. The philosophical approach based on the way we discover consciousness functioning (called noesis) and that to which consciousness is directed (called the noema) is obviously not the same as the empirical science that attempts to base itself on publicly discernible behavior and often refuses to acknowledge that consciousness is an important source of knowledge. We can include moral experience in our understanding of ethics without blurring the distinction between philosophy and psychology. We run a risk of making philosophical ethics so abstract as to have little bearing on human life if our fear of contaminating philosophy with bits of moral psychology makes us fortify the borders between the two disciplines. Philosophy and psychology must rub shoulders, even walk in the same path from time to time, to keep us from making our philosophy so much neater than life that it cannot come to grips with actual human living. Phenomenology can give to our understanding of moral experience insights to which empirical psychology and analytical philosophy do not have access.

How should we proceed? A first step is an examination of two types of moral thinking, both of which have been called reflection. One kind of thinking leads to an impasse in moral reasoning, an impasse that makes it impossible for us to let knowledge enrich and guide our understanding of moral obligation. The other kind of moral reflection brings together knowledge and obligation, and that is the mode of reflection I wish to explore, to see how to use it and how to justify its use.

NOTES

1. Charles L. Stevenson, *Fact and Values* (New Haven: Yale University Press, 1963), esp. ch. 2; R. M. Hare, *The Language of Morals* (London: Oxford University Press, 1952), esp. ch. 1.

2. G. E. Moore, *Principia Ethica* (Cambridge: Cambridge University Press, 1903), preface and chapter 1; also H. A. Pritchard, "Does Moral Philosophy Rest on a Mistake?" *Mind* 21 (1912).

3. David Hume, *An Inquiry Concerning Human Understanding,* pt. 1, sec. 1, and appendix; David Hume, *A Treatise of Human Nature,* bk. 2, pt. 3, sec. 3; bk. 3, pt. 1, sec. 1.

4. G. E. Moore, *Principia Ethica*, preface and chapter 1; also W. K. Frankena, "The Naturalistic Fallacy," *Mind* 48 (1939).

5. Kenneth R. Pahel, "Steven Pepper's Ethical Empiricism," *The Southern Journal of Philosophy* 5 (1967): 48–58.

Chapter Two

Finding Moral Obligation in Primal Experience

There are different ways to reflect about life, the world, and oneself. Some philosophers have meant by moral reflection a type of thinking that turns immediately into abstract and theoretical tracks, setting about putting things into categories, making relative and analytical judgments, and seeking familiar patterns. Reflection need not be pursued in this way, however; it can peruse the matters that come to attention, seeing the individual things as fully as possible in their concreteness and also in their contexts. Comparisons and classifications can be allowed to come in their due time, without forcing them. The first type of reflection, which is primarily reflecting on ideas and concepts, is the mode that gives rise to puzzles and questions about knowledge, values, and moral duty. I call it abstract reflection and contrast it with a kind of phenomenological approach that I call concrete reflection.

THE LIMITS OF ABSTRACT REFLECTION

Abstract reflection focuses on individual things and parts of things as separate entities, whether it addresses perceptible objects, concepts, or experiences themselves. It tries to reduce things to their simplest natures for purposes of classification. This mode of reflection is highly theoretical and it tends to simplification and abstraction. Its goal is to understand a thing in the simplest and most abstract concept of it that reflection upon it can attain. This kind of reflection has been widely practiced, especially since René Descartes (1596–1650), the founder of Continental Rationalism, made it a critical part of his philosophical method and Gottfried W. Leibniz (1646–1716), German mathemetician and philosopher, made it part of his method.[1] John Locke

(1632–1704), noted British empiricist, reinforced this emphasis on isolated simple natures with his claim that all knowledge is based on simple ideas that enter the mind (conceptualized as a dark room into which nothing but simple perceptions can enter) devoid of any context.[2]

It seems that this analysis of isolated atoms of information is the only kind of reflection some thinkers know. Despite its popularity, however, in seeking to discover the nature of things in separation from other things, it gives rise to theoretical problems in ethics and value theory. These theoretical problems, such as the "is/ought" impasse, make a connection between knowledge and obligation difficult to establish. They tend to separate knowledge from duty and duty from action. One way abstract reflection does this is through its tendency to be analytic when it turns toward individual things, trying to grasp these things in themselves, because this is trying to understand them apart from the contexts in which they are discovered, the contexts that give them much of their meaning and importance.

The isolation of matters from their contexts facilitates one sort of examination and description, but it makes the understanding of values difficult. Within the mode of abstract reflection, it is easy to doubt that value can be anything more than sentiment. With the connections with other matters severed, description of a thing is limited to only certain aspects of it, usually its physical characteristics. What Locke called primary qualities are perceived as the only real aspects of a thing.

Abstract reflection is reductionistic in seeing things out of their context in our experience in order to see them in their simple natures. These ways of seeing make for simplicity and a kind of clarity, but they do not help us see things in their fullness of being or their richness of value. This mode of reflection also seeks to understand things by placing them in categories. The categories come mainly from previous intellectual formulations. This facilitates interpreting things in terms of an accepted metaphysical framework or an established worldview, but this is not the same as grasping the significance of things fully and accurately. At times abstract modes of reflection actually stimulate criticism of the categories into which things are sorted, but this is not what usually happens. Abstract reflection leads to a problem of misinterpretation of things and to a problem of dichotomies and logical impasses that another mode of reflection would not have created.

When we reflect upon worldly objects, knowledge of the world, values, and moral obligations as separated matters, we try to know and understand them apart from other things. One result of this is that we are trying to grasp the significance of things apart from what gives them much of their significance. Another result is that, having torn things in our lived worlds apart, we are not able to put them together again. Descartes's step in philosophical method following analysis was to put back together all the small parts separated by analysis, and deduction was seen as the way to arrive at certainty through this process. Leaving aside the question of whether Descartes ever used his method successfully, we can see that deduction remains for many thinkers the reasoning process of choice, the paradigm of rational thinking. Along with deduction, induction was needed since it is the only way to establish generalizations about matters of fact. With philosophers using deduction and induction to put together the analyzed fragments of a world, moral reasoning was faced with the "is/ought" impasse. Factual information was allowed only a minor role in moral reasoning. Knowledge could do little in establishing basic moral principles.

Basic moral principles simply had to be adopted, as a matter of choice. Since there was no way to demonstrate that our basic moral principles were the correct moral principles, morality seemed to be a matter of personal opinion. This turn toward subjectivism seemed inevitable. If morality is all a matter of personal choice, it is unseemly for one person to fault the choices of another. Yet we are uneasy with subjectivism. We want to call some behaviors into question, while we want to encourage other behaviors. We are not satisfied with the cynic's claim that wanting to make moral judgment is just a meddlesome desire to exert power over others or resentment that someone is enjoying what we do not enjoy. We need to look closely at the supposed separation of morality from knowledge and rational thought.

The "is/ought" impasse is an example of the separation between knowledge and moral obligation, now a widely accepted view in ethical theory that a moral norm cannot be derived from factual knowledge. To argue, for example, that certain changes in governmental programs would cause increased poverty among some social classes, therefore it would be immoral to legislate the changes, might seem like sound morality to many people, but the argument is not valid. To be a valid argument there must be a normative general principle among the premises, along with the factual premises about the effects of the proposed changes. This premise might be that government should promote the general welfare by trying to eliminate, and certainly not act to exacerbate, poverty. Well, what is the problem? This premise is easy enough to supply. The problem lies in justifying the normative premise. We know how to justify the factual premises about the effect of governmental policies, even if there is some disagreement about it, but how do we justify a general moral principle? The "is/ought impasse" prevents us from using factual information to prove the moral premise.

In the previous chapter I claimed that there are ways around this "is/ought impasse." We need to be clear about this; there does not seem to be any way around the impasse if we insist on using deduction and induction as our way to seek justification for our moral principles. The prohibition against deduction of moral principles from factual premises seems to be logically sound. Several philosophers attempted to give examples of "ought" statements derived from factual premises. An example offered by John Searle is not generally accepted as successful in breaking the impasse; it uses premises incorporating the social institution of promising, and the "institutional facts" used by Searle already include moral principles. Max Black's example logically derives an "ought" statement, but this "ought" is a practical matter, stating that a person ought to build a fire in the stove in order to keep warm; it does not support a moral obligation to keep warm. It might be silly for a cold person to suffer the cold stoically, but it would not be immoral in ordinary circumstances. If there is a danger of freezing to death, there could be a moral issue involved, but the duty would be to preserve one's life. Lighting a fire is just one practical means of meeting a moral obligation. It might be more practical to be picked up by the rescue helicopter hovering overhead. Moral obligations are not quite like practical means of achieving what one wants. I do not think that moral "oughts" are as radically different from practical "oughts" as some moral philosophers seem to think, but moral obligations do have a morally significant context that is lacking in purely practical cases. It is the moral significance that Black's example does not provide.[3] There are ways to approach moral thinking apart from deductive reasoning, however, and I will talk about them later when explaining concrete reflection.

Abstract and analytical reflection creates problems in understanding values, as well as understanding moral principles. The justification of values has proved to be problematical within the analytical mode of reflection. When values were separated from other values and subjected to close scrutiny, these values were like lonely frightened prisoners being tortured in a back room. They did not stand up to inspection very well. They were at a significant disadvantage separated from the contexts in which they would have meaning, being understood abstractly, as "honesty," "beauty," or "friendship." They also ran afoul of a logical impasse, the "fact/value dichotomy," which is similar to the "is/ought impasse." Values cannot be defended through logical argument with only factual premises. There appeared to be an unsurpassable barrier between factual information and values. A subjectivistic theory of value seemed to be called for. Even now many, perhaps most, philosophers will state as something that is beyond doubt that values are subjective, unlike facts that can be known objectively. There are better ways to seek an understanding of value, and more of that later.

Why does the abstract mode of reflection create theoretical problems for ethics, value theory, and the making of moral decisions? The problems come because abstract reflection begins with separating aspects of our lived worlds, separating values from factual matters and separating values from other values. When our lived worlds are fragmented in this way, it is virtually impossible to put together again that which was together in our most primal constitution of a lived world.

Maurice Merleau-Ponty (1908–1961), a leading developer of Existential Phenomenology, which stresses experience of the life world, criticizes the "objectivistic ontology" that we inherited from Descartes, an ontology that maintains a doubting of human experience, holding it suspect, often dismissing it as subjective. He directs us to a reflection on "that primordial being which is not yet the subject-being nor the object-being." [4]

CONCRETE REFLECTION

When we approach the worldly things and our own lives in the world with concrete reflection, we see matters from a perspective different from that of abstract, theoretical reflection. Concrete reflection is not initially theoretical, but a mode of nonjudgmental observation. We are not hastening to reach conclusions, comparisons, and categorizations. We are observing, not speculating. What we are doing is examining our experiences of the objects presented to us.

In the descriptive mode of concrete reflection we do not experience some of the distinctions and separations that abstract reflection imposes upon our engagement with the world. An important aspect of this is that the lonely self, the self set apart from all things as a pure observer who is not a part of the world and radically distinct from every other self, is not found in descriptive reflection on our primal openness to the world. This pre-thetic world, in which what Merleau-Ponty called intellectualist analysis has not yet led us to see ourselves as separate from all things, presents us with a unified experience very different from the Cartesian world of separated subjects and objects.

Merleau-Ponty elucidates the radical alteration that analytic reflection makes in consciousness of worldly objects. Within this kind of reflection we make the objects of which we were conscious in concrete reflection into mere elements of consciousness. We are no longer reflecting upon a world given to us, but perceiving and thinking about a construction that lacks much of the significance of original awareness. He said, "we miss . . . the basic operation which infuses significance into the sensible."[5]

Concrete reflection does not pull apart and treat as separate those things that are found together in a person's experience of a world. This is the world as we are directly aware of it, in contrast to a theoretical notion of the world.

Concrete reflection describes what is given in experience of the world. It is not analytical and abstract, and it tries to avoid letting theoretical notions distort the way the world is experienced. It favors the concrete constitution of particular things, not abstractions and generalities. This is not to say that a phenomenological mode of reflection precludes all generalization, but it does not start with generalization, and is always more assured of particulars than of generalities. It does not preclude the use of argument, but argument is not its primary goal and cannot take the place of reflective description. The conclusion of any argument must be tested against reflective description, a way of heeding Husserl's admonition to return to the matters themselves.

The descriptive mode of reflection eventually incorporates generalization and explanation, but the search for these does not drive us toward hasty conclusions. Several aspects of concrete reflection show how description moves toward generalization and explanation.

One aspect is the unity of experience in this mode of reflection. As we reflect on the world we realize that our horizons of perception are flexible. We can focus narrowly upon the more immediate context, or we can see matters in a much wider context. In the wider context we can consider other similar matters. With the aid of memory, our reflection within the broad context includes the naming and grouping of things. It is important to see that we do not paint our world by a kind of intellectual pointillism. We are not seeing the world the way one might look at a newspaper picture, seeing not the picture but the dots alone as real. In what Merleau-Ponty described as "the upsurge of a true and accurate world," we are not looking at bits of sense data that we must make into a picture. Experience does not give us here a "pure sensation," here an "atom of feeling." The world brings to us matters in a context.[6]

Perceiving whole contexts in concrete reflection enables us to progress from the particular to the general, and it provides a context for seeing the connection between description and explanation. Since we see some things as associated with other things, including seeing some as causally related to others, an element of explanation enters our reflection. At this point, we must be careful not to let preestablished schema override our attention to the matters themselves. A critical attitude toward interpretive schema and frequent return to the matters themselves is an important difference between concrete reflection and abstract, intellectualizing reflection.

An important observation about our awareness of the world with which we are engaged is that our reflection does not find a firm separation of factual information from meaning and value. Merleau-Ponty describes the most primordial lived-world as a world charged with meaning. In this mode of reflection we can become aware of the value that an object has for us, for example, its beauty or its usefulness, before we take heed of its physical properties. We do not measure the roses or analyze their aroma. We see them and smell them and recognize that they are good. This is important in seeing the way to avoid the "is/ought" impasse through not approaching moral judgment by way of deductive argument, as we will see later.

Seeking the basis of moral judgment apart from logical argument will not be welcomed by some philosophers, especially those who expect a foundationalist support for ethics. I can understand their desire for a system of ethics grounded in irrefutable arguments. For centuries, this has been what many philosophers have sought. This goal for ethics has, however, been the source of frustration and failure, and this has led to unnecessary skepticism about the possibility of finding a rational basis for ethics.

In chapter 7, I will return to this matter and defend the adequacy of a non-foundationalist approach to ethics. Now I will point out that what I propose is not as radical as it might seem. American Pragmatism and the "good reasons" school of ethics have shown that principles of morality do not need to be supported by deductive argument. In the special field of environmental ethics, there are several philosophers who show that moral issues of the natural environment can be informed by knowledge of ecology even though the moral principles used are not deduced from the scientific knowledge.

Holmes Rolston III, who has done extensive work on ethical theory as it is used in environmental ethics, describes the relationship between ecological knowledge and awareness of obligation to the environment as immediate. He writes that the environmental "ought" is not derived from the ecological "is," but is discovered simultaneously with it. He says, " . . . the values seem to be there as soon as the facts are fully in." [7]

Arne Naess, who is widely recognized for his contributions to an ethic based on ecological knowledge, holds that environmental ethics is not a product of deduction. He holds that the principles of environmental ethics are not derived by logic or induction from ecological science. He says that knowledge of ecology and the experience of environmental fieldworkers have "suggested, inspired, and fortified the perspective of the Deep Ecology movement." [8] I believe these philosophers and others are correct in finding the basis of environmental ethics apart from a foundation supported by formal logic, and I believe their insight applies to ethical thinking generally, not just to one branch of ethics.

The metaethical approach that I support begins with the concrete mode of reflection on the aspects of our experience of engagement with the world in which facts, values, obligations, and volition are together. They are not yet separated by constitution as facts distinct from values or obligations distinct from values and volition. Starting with a mode of reflection that does not begin with these aspects of the lived-world already separated from each other, we find together in our most primal experience, in the givenness of the world to us, aspects of experience that moral philosophers have been trying to bring together through logical argument. We eventually separate these elements of primitive experience when we constitute matters according to familiar categories and make our grasp of these things more general, abstract, and less immediate, but we should not forget that originally we found them together. When we reflect on our lived-worlds we find that there is no separation of factual information from meaning and value. That the primordial lived world is "charged with meaning," as Merleau-Ponty described it, that worldly objects can have a value for us which we recognize without deriving the value from physical properties, has ethical implications which we will explain later.[9]

The conjunction of facts and values was realized by the psychologist Abraham Maslow and other researchers whom he cites.[10] Maslow describes a "fusion" of fact and value in experience. He cites as an example of this fusion his experience of learning the medical use of hypnosis. He writes that he came to realize the value of hypnosis and knew, as his knowledge of hypnosis grew, that he should learn how to use it. He says that his realizing the value of this medical technique did not come from logical argument, but was a growing sense of value and obligation fused with his factual learning. I believe Maslow had an important insight, although I do not think "fusion" is the ideal word to describe what he is writing about. To call these elements fused suggests that they are so strongly bonded that they cannot be separated, and we do separate them as we constitute various aspects of experience. Perhaps the important point is that we need not separate them so completely that one aspect of the original experience does not affect others, and it is important that a connection between the factual, valuational, deontic, and volitional aspects of our lived worlds is something discovered, not deduced. The nature of these aspects of experience and their discovery will be developed further in the chapters that follow.

Lest this insight be dismissed as being psychology, not a matter of philosophy, as if a boundary between these two disciplines were as distinct and well protected as some philosophers seem to believe, we need to see that a nondeductive connection between factual knowledge and moral obligation is not a new and radical idea in moral philosophy. Maurice Mandelbaum wrote extensively on this connection, and John Rawls also recognized it.[11]

A phenomenological explanation of awareness of moral obligation, starting with the presence of factual and valuational matter together in the person's lived-world, the world most immediately given to consciousness, the world as experienced rather than as understood abstractly and theoretically, provides us the clearest comprehension of an undeduced awareness of moral obligation. With consciousness of fact and value come an awareness of, approval of, and desire for some states of affairs and aversion to others. Volition, as well as value, is found in our primal constitution of the world with which we are engaged.[12]

When we begin our moral thinking within the mode of concrete phenomenological reflection, we no longer have as our main problem bringing together factual information and moral obligation. We do not begin with an "is/ought" problem. The impasse between factual thinking and moral thinking comes when our thinking begins with a separation of factual matters from valuational and deontic matters at the very start of the process of decision making.

Justification of moral judgments is not complete at the stage in which we recognize the union of the several aspects of thought and action in our most original constitution of a world. The problem of justification is a very different problem, however, from that with which metaethics has been struggling. All of our constitutions are subject to question and need to be justified, but the justification of moral and valuational matters is not radically different from other aspects of judgment. We need not begin with factual judgments to which we give a primary and seldom questioned credence, and on the basis of which we must justify our moral judgments.

If the reader is troubled at this point that I have not given convincing arguments for accepting the givenness in experience of valuational and moral matters, let it be noted that I have not tried to give arguments at all. The method of phenomenological reflection employed does not attempt to argue. What it does is describe, and the basis of discussion is the reader's recognition of a similar primal constitution of a lived-world. Reference to other moral philosophers whose approach is similar to mine is not meant as a way to support my case on their authority. These references are used to illustrate the method more clearly and to acknowledge my indebtedness to these thinkers.

As a basis of dialogue, I invite those not already familiar with concrete reflection to engage in this mode of reflection. The experiences I remember are probably similar to those of other people. Elsewhere I have written of experiencing a large body of water for the first time and of coming upon a large bed of tulips.[13] What I realize in reflecting on these experiences is that valuational, affective, and volitional factors were immediate features of the experiences. I did not first become aware of the natural properties of the objects of experience. I did not begin with sizes, shapes, and designated colors, then go on to figure out what I felt about the objects. The first thing realized about Mobile Bay was that I was thrilled by it and glad to be beside it. Later I could relate the thrill to its size, color, and wave motion. I was a child then, but even now the lapping of waves on a shore gives me a feeling that I get even before I think about waves and sand. The beauty of the tulips struck me forcefully before I thought about specific colors and shapes or even thought that the flowers were tulips.

The connection between the factual and valuational aspects of the experiences I have described does not lend itself to a simple scheme of dependency of one aspect on another. The feelings and values were not unrelated to the physical aspects, but this relationship cannot be schematized as an argument. It is not a matter of premises and a conclusion. It is not (1) I see dynamic waters as far as eye can see, (2) I am stirred pleasurably by such waters, therefore I am stirred by this bay. I would not be thrilled had the bay been strikingly smaller, but somehow the premises do not entail the conclusion. Imagine that I was a farmer whose farm by the Mississippi River was now submerged under dynamic waters that stretch as far as eye can see. I would not have been pleasurably thrilled. In looking back upon a striking experience, we are tempted to simplify the connection between physical aspects and the feelings and valuations by putting it into a familiar pattern, but any such connection is not part of the original experience.

I believe everyone has similar experiences, and what I am asking for is concrete reflection upon them. It might be difficult to withhold analysis until the experience is described, but it should be worth the effort. The realization of factual and valuational matters united with feelings and volitions is not limited to experiences of vast things or brilliantly colored things. Seeing a baby in a crib, seeing a child playing, seeing a kitten trying to catch a ball of yarn, seeing a small flower trying to grow in a hole in the pavement, and other simple things can speak to us of tenderness and joy in the presence of life. Unpleasant sights can speak to us of pain, frustration, loss, and grief that we can feel before we catalogue the material facts before us, and which we probably remember far more vividly than the material details.

Since concrete reflection upon our lived worlds is just the beginning of the justification of our moral stances, we must employ additional tools to decide which constitutions of our lived-worlds are important and which are defensible. What we describe might not be correct or adequate. I am not claiming that just feeling a certain way justifies moral or other sorts of valuation. No matter how assured one is of a moral intuition, this putative insight must be tested.

It is for this reason that I do not want my approach that begins with concrete reflection to be confused with Max Scheler's approach to material values, an approach that is generally recognized as an intuitionist approach.[14] My thought has been enriched by Scheler (1874–1928), a moral philosopher influenced by, but critical of, Husserl, and I appreciate especially his recognition of the moral importance of material values. I am skeptical of Scheler's intuition of the different ranks of "value-modalities." Placing at the low end of the scale of values "sensible feeling," with values "correlated with vital feeling" higher, but below "spiritual values" and all of these lower than values related to the holy is critically important to his ethical theory. For Scheler material values are related to good and evil through this "order of rank among non-formal values." He wrote, "our willing is 'good' insofar as it chooses the higher value lying in inclinations." [15] My reflection does not find these ranks of types of valuation, and my justification of basing moral obligation on material values cannot be stated as formally as Scheler's.

Not only do I not support Scheler's ranking of kinds of valuation apart from specific contexts, I do not accept the idea of intuitive a priori knowledge of values of the sort he claims.[16] Concrete reflection does not give me intuitions of the sort claimed by Scheler.

There are a number of reasons for rejecting intuitionism as a basis for ethics. Many thinkers believe that what seems to be an intuition is actually of social origin, an internalization of social influences. This may well be the most likely explanation of the origin of intuitions, but even if it is not and the origin of intuitions is not so easily dealt with, intuitionism faces a serious difficulty.

My main objection to basing morality on intuitions is that this approach makes strong claims in a way that stops the moral dialogue, leaving no more to be said and nothing more to be investigated. A claim of intuitive a priori knowledge leaves us with the alternatives of full acceptance or total rejection.

If someone finds in concrete reflection something different from what I find, I see this as an opportunity for mutual exploration. Intuitionism would not allow for this valuable moral dialectic. Even after moral values are generally accepted, there is still work to be done in making moral judgments.

Concrete reflection can show that much logical thought begins with distinctions and separations that have been taken for granted, but these are not as basic as we might have believed. We are freed from the necessity of joining facts and values in the face of a logical impasse. We must still proceed to justify our moral judgments, but what we must do is different from the task usually thought to be demanded by metaethical considerations. We have some important tools to use in justifying our moral principles, and we will look at these in the following chapter.

NOTES

1. Descartes, *Discourse on Method*, pt. 2 (550[19]); Leibniz, *On the Universal Science: Characteristic* XV.

2. John Locke, *An Essay Concerning Human Understanding,* pt. 2, especially chapters 1–11.3.

3. John R. Searle, "How to Derive 'Ought' from 'Is,'" *The Philosophical Review* 73 (January 1964); Max Black, "The Gap Between 'Is' and 'Should,'" *Philosophical Review* 73 (January 1964).

4. Maurice Merleau-Ponty, *The Visible and the Invisible Followed by Working Notes* (Evanston, Ill.: Northwestern University Press, 1968), 106, 183; also *Themes from the Lectures at the College of France,* 1952–1960, trans. John O'Neill (Evanston, Ill.: Northwestern University Press, 1970), 65–66.

5. Maurice Merleau-Ponty, *The Phenomenology of Perception*, trans. Colin Smith (New York: Humanities Press, 1962), 5.

6. Merleau-Ponty, *The Phenomenology of Perception*, 4–5, 21, 24, 52.

7. Holmes Rolston III, "Is There an Ecological Ethic?" *Ethics* 85 (1975): 93–109.

8. Arne Naess, "The Shallow and the Deep, Long-Range Ecology Movement. A Summary," *Inquiry* 16 (1973): 95–100.

9. See note 5.

10. Abraham H. Maslow, "Fusions of Facts and Values," *American Journal of Psycho-Analysis* 23 (1963): 120–35.

11. Maurice Mandelbaum, *The Phenomenology of Moral Experience* (Baltimore: Johns Hopkins University Press, 1969), especially chapters 2, 5, and 6; also John Rawls, "Outline of a Decision Procedure for Ethics," *Philosophical Review* 66 (1957): 177–97.

12. Lester Embree, "Some Noetico-Noematic Analyses of Action and Practical Life," in *The Phenomenology of the Noema*, ed. J. J. Drummond and Lester Embree, (Dordrecht, The Netherlands: Kluwer Academic Publishers, 1992), 198–200; see also Lester Embree, "Phenomenology of Action for Ecosystemic Health or How to Tend One's Own Garden," and Don E. Marietta, Jr., "Reflection and Environmental Activism," in *Environmental Philosophy and Environmental Activism*, ed. Don E. Marietta, Jr. and Lester Embree (Lanham, Md.: Rowman & Littlefield, 1995), 51–66, 79–97.

13. Don E. Marietta, Jr., *For People and the Planet: Holism and Humanism in Environmental Ethics* (Philadelphia: Temple University Press, 1995), 90; also "Reflection and Environmental Activism," in *Environmental Philosophy and Environmental Activism*, ed. Don E. Marietta, Jr., and Lester Embree (Lanham, Md.: Rowman & Littlefield, 1995), 84–85; also "Back to Earth with Reflection and Ecology," in *Eco-Phenomenolody: Back to The Earth Itself*," ed. Charles S. Brown and Ted Toadvine (Albany: State University of New York Press, 2003), 121–35.

14. See Manfred S. Frings, *Max Scheler* (Pittsburgh: Duquesne University Press, 1965). See also Phliip Blosser, *Scheler's Critique of Kant's Ethics* (Athens: Ohio University Press, 1995 also "Ethics in Scheler," in *Encyclopedia of Phenomenology*, ed. Lester Embree et al. (Dordrecht: Kluwer Academic Publishers, 1997).

15. Max Scheler, *Formalism in Ethics and Non-Formal Ethics of Values* (Evanston, Ill.: Northwestern University Press, 1973): 25, 42, 106–8.

16. Scheler, *Formalism in Ethics,* 104–10.

Chapter Three

Making Moral Judgments

Concrete reflection on our most original constitutions of our lived worlds gives us only a start toward making moral judgments. It is an important start, in which we can see that elements of fact, value, a sense of obligation, and volition are discovered to be together initially and not separate and unrelated matters that we must unite by discovering some logical relationship between them. We must acknowledge, however, the possibility that our most primal constitutions can be mistaken. We must move beyond this basic level of reflection, reflection that seeks to describe, not to judge and make systematic the elements of basic experience.

When we advance beyond our first concrete reflection, we do not need to fall into the same patterns of justification that led to impasses in other approaches to metaethics. We need not abandon the basic insight that elements of factual and moral knowledge are joined in our primal experience of the world. We must, however, question our valuations, as well as the affective, factual, and volitional aspects of our constitutions. We should not assume that the factual elements have a greater surety or are somehow more basic than the other elements. We cannot take the factual aspects for granted and seek a way to make the factual justify the other elements of our experience.

How can we justify our moral insights without turning to analytic, objectifying reflection and logical argument? There may be more than one valid approach a person can take at this point; it is not my purpose to refute or denigrate other ethical approaches that offer guidance in the formation of moral judgments. I believe some of them are more helpful than others but that some of them offer especially valuable insight into the human condition, especially the moral aspect of human living. In the chapter on moral pluralism my reasons for this openness will become clearer. I take as my philosophical task the explanation of a phenomenological approach able to support sound moral thinking. I believe it is stronger than other approaches; therefore I devote my efforts to clarifying and advocating it.

This approach begins with the basic insight of a union of the fundamental elements of experience in our most primal engagement with the world. It then goes on to use some tools of judgment, especially intersubjectivity, a recognition of fittingness between factual and moral aspects of the world, and criticism of the individual worldviews underlying our judgments. Intersubjectivity is not limited to agreement among subjects about the physical features of the world; it can inform us about judgments of value more richly than we usually realize. The fittingness we will look for is that between specific situations and the behaviors that the situations call for. Individual worldviews play a significant part in our constitution of those situations that we believe to be morally significant. We do not need to accept these individual perspectives as inexplicable givens, but we can examine the source of our worldviews and make critical judgments about their adequacy.

INTERSUBJECTIVITY

In using these tools of judgment, we do not abandon concrete reflection. Even though we are now on a more theoretical and more reasoned level of thought, we need to hold on to concreteness in observation. We should not abandon the matters themselves in a pursuit of intellectual schemes.

Intersubjectivity is not to be confused with mere popular opinion. The intersubjectivity we seek should not be a kind of opinion polling; we can place greater weight on opinions that have come through concrete reflection than we can on opinions picked up along the way without serious reflection and examination.

The determination of fittingness requires concrete reflection; fittingness in respect to some preconceived doctrine is not what we seek. In the same way, we must not let evaluation of individual worldviews be dominated by a theoretical perspective that was reached by abstract reflection alone.

We are accustomed to relying heavily on intersubjectivity to support factual claims about objects and situations in the world. Intersubjectivity is the nearest thing we have to objectivity, that is, knowledge that is free of the influence of individuals and society. We now realize that there are no "brute facts" that are not colored in any degree by the observers of the events described or the society to which the observers belong. We sometimes call objective the judgments that are supported by virtually unanimous agreement. We would do well, I think, to avoid merely designating factual claims as objective, since we can and should be explicit about our reasons for accepting a claim. One such reason is a high degree of intersubjective verification.

We are wise to be careful about knowledge claims that lack wide support, and we must assess supporting opinions critically. Some people are better prepared to make factual judgments because of education, training in research methods, a discriminating attitude, and freedom from obvious prejudice or obsequious dependence on conventional notions. There is also a moral aspect to the ability to make sound judgments; obvious self-interest and a lack of sufficient discipline to avoid wishful thinking make us suspicious of some claims.

Even though intersubjective verification is not just a matter of counting noses, and we might be accused of being elitist in giving more weight to the factual reports of some people, it is intersubjectivity on which we rely. Idiosyncratic constitutions of the factual aspect of the world and the peculiar ideas of a cultural group could be true, but we trust those claims about the world that have significant support, and intersubjectivity is our most trusted source of support for factual reports.

In spite of our reliance on intersubjectivity in supporting claims about the physical nature of the world, moral philosophers and other morally concerned people have made very little use of intersubjectivity in support of value claims and moral judgments. People have tended to see agreement about nonfactual matters as fads, fashions, sectarian doctrines, and other things considered trivial compared to factual information. It is regrettable that intersubjectivity has been neglected in dealing with moral judgments and values. The neglect was not a result of a paucity of agreement about these matters. Within our culture there is a great deal of agreement about values and appropriate behavior. What we have done is focus our attention on the areas of disagreement and judge from them that nonfactual judgments are matters of mere opinion, arbitrary liking and disliking of certain behaviors and dispositions. Minor disagreements in issues about which we have considerable agreement are treated as major conflicts. Anything short of complete agreement is seen as another example of the groundlessness of judgments of value and conduct.

A basic disagreement does not show that both of two conflicting moral stances are arbitrary expressions of baseless opinion. Often we reject one view and accept another because one lacks the evidence of thought shown by the other. This is what we should do. The belief that girls lack the mental ability to master difficult subjects and therefore should be taught only domestic skills does not stand on all fours with the moral claim that full educational opportunities should be provided for girls as well as boys. That some people disagree does not weaken the case for equal education. The wide agreement among knowledgeable people that girls should receive full educational advantages is a strong point in favor of a policy of equal educational opportunity.

If we pay as much attention to the agreements as to the disagreements, we will find more intersubjective agreement over values than we have recognized. We will find that we share more values than we knew. This should not surprise us. Our culture would not be as strong as it is if we disagreed as strongly as we tend to assume when we discuss values theoretically. Even within the areas of very strong disagreement we have significant agreement. It is because of these areas of agreement that our disputes are significant. When we argue about the superiority of public or private education, the arguments of both sides rest on an agreement that education is a valuable function of the society. When Mother talks of going to the doctor and Sis holds out for acupuncture, they are both committed to the value of good health. Are there any important disputes that do not have such a foundation in agreement?

We need to reflect on the disagreements between serious-minded people, seeing clearly the aspects of divergence and the areas of commonality. If we do this, we will get a truer picture of people's thought. Moreover, we then can see that disagreements are not always nugatory.

Disagreements do not rob us of value. In fact, they allow us to have a culture that is varied and rich. We do not worry over the fact that the local art museum has a floor of traditional works of art and a floor of contemporary works of art. We see it all as art, even though some of us enjoy one floor more than another. We see it all as evidence of a commitment to art. My friends who do not care for ballet may be strong supporters of the opera. The ballet people seem to understand people liking opera. Why do they? For one thing, both are developments of musical culture. The friends who rave about Thai food do not consider the devotees of Italian food weird or misguided; both enjoy and value good and interesting food. I have even come to understand why some people enjoy rock music concerts. It involves many of the same values I find in opera and ballet: music, spectacle, admiration of skill, excitement, and fellowship with fellow enjoyers. The value differences between the rock music people and me does not seem as great as it once did. Perhaps we should learn to see some of our moral disputes as evidence of a commitment to morality.

We might expect some strong agreements within a cultural group, but those who argue for the arbitrariness of values use intercultural differences as their trump card. I now see this as a bluff more than a legitimate play. Even interculturally there seems to be more agreement than disagreement. The differences may be more interesting than the agreements, and they demand our attention. The agreements seem rather obvious and trivial, so we tend to minimize them. What we take for triviality, however, may indicate that the areas of agreement are what is really basic. Some anthropologists and other students of cultures have claimed that there are basic shared values in very different cultures. I believe they are right about this. Dashikis, polo shirts, serapes, and loincloths seem to be concessions to different climates.

The use of clothing or ornamentation of the body seems to be universal. What is the basic value here? I feel fortunate to live in an area that blends many cultures. It is easy for me to enjoy the things valued by many countries. Am I wrong to feel sorry for the people who are so culture-bound that they have a narrow range of good things to choose? No, these people are deprived of something I can easily enjoy, things they too would enjoy having available if they had been exposed to them soon enough.

Lest the reader be drawing the conclusion that I am a sybarite who places an excessive value on dietary pleasures and cultural enjoyments, let us see that intercultural agreements in value are in basic areas of life. Prominent among these are moral values. We should not make light of the virtually universal disapproval of lying to, stealing from, and causing people bodily harm. There are peoples who disapprove only of harmful acts toward a narrow range of people, such as fellow members of a tribe, but these are peoples who have yet to develop along lines in which all cultures with adequate resources seem to grow.

Even when there are cultural differences in moral standards, these can often be accounted for or are not of primary importance. Also, we need to be careful not to classify as moral disagreements differences that are not really moral differences, but are merely cultural matters of dress, diet, and social arrangement. The presence of some moral disagreements, along with significant agreements, is what we should expect. People in some cultures seem to place less value on individual lives than do people in other cultures, but they do value life. Even if they seem to value pride, dignity, or reputation more than we value them, we also value pride, dignity, and reputation. The differences are real and undeniable, but it is wrong to see these disagreements as an indication that all valuation is mere whimsy.

The intersubjectivity that can contribute to the credibility of moral values and insights must not be narrowly bound to one culture. Spending a significant amount of time with people of other cultures, sharing their lives and coming to understand something of their lives, contributes greatly to one's ability to engage creatively in concrete reflection. This does not require that one be a world traveler. Reading and studying about other cultures as reported by sympathetic writers can contribute to a person's intercultural enrichment. I have found the novels of Tony Hillerman, set on the Navaho reservation in New Mexico, have contributed to my understanding of Navaho culture. His *Sacred Clowns* led to an especially insightful reflection.

A subplot in Hillerman's novel tells that Clement Hoski, returning home drunk from a party, hit and killed a pedestrian. He did not realize that it was a person he had hit until he learned of the death the next day. Hoski drove to the radio station in Farmington and used the microphone kept in the lobby for the making of public announcements to confess that he had killed the old man walking beside Navajo Route 1. He said that he was sorry, and he was going to make restitution to the man's family. Then he drove away without giving his name.

Sammie Yazzie, in charge of the station at the time, saw Hoski's dirty old pickup. He could not read the license plate, but noticed a bumper sticker on the tailgate, "ERNIE IS THE GREATEST." Yazzie described how the man who made the announcement dressed, including a cap with the bill bent, and he said the man smelled like onions.

Jim Chee, a Navaho tribal policeman studying to be a hataalii, a custodian of Navaho lore and a leader of the traditional songs at ceremonials, surmised that the man who smelled like onions worked for the Navaho Agricultural Industries. Chee located a man of the right age, wearing a cap with the bent bill. The man did not drive a pickup, but rode with a car pool. Chee traced him to his house and stopped down the road to see if he could see a pickup.

A boy got off the school bus for special education children. Chee recognized that he was a victim of fetal alcohol syndrome. The friendly boy stopped to talk and admire Chee's pickup. Chee learned that his grandfather, who kept an old green pickup behind his house, had adopted him and looked after him. The boy said his name was Ernie. A few days later Chee met Ernie at the school bus stop and gave him a bumper sticker saying "I have the world champion grandson!" He instructed Ernie to have his grandfather place it over the old sticker.

In explaining to Jane Pete, his half-Navaho girlfriend, who was not raised on the reservation, why he did not arrest Hoski, Chee explained the Navaho concept of justice. He explained to Jane that he respects his people's religious and traditional ways. He learned as a boy the Navaho concept of justice and retribution in dealing with a person who fails to act according to tribal expectations. This concept is not like the "eye for an eye" approach that expects to cause the offender a degree of pain comparable to the offense. The Navaho approach is that the offender sits down with the family hurt by his actions to figure the damage and how to make good their loss. That is the way to restore harmony between families, and the offender is returned to harmony with the community, is made beautiful again. If the offender continues to do harmful things, the fault is his, and he must be handled by a way like standard American justice, but the purpose is to heal him.[1]

A Unitarian Universalist minister friend of mine described in a sermon the practice of an African tribe. The offender is seated in the center of a circle, and the people of the tribe tell him of good things he has done. In this way he is led to grasp his place in the tribe and the value a life lived according to tribal standards.

Reflection on Hillerman's story of Navaho justice and the African tribe's handling of an offender gave me a new perspective on justice. Part of the Navaho concept, reconciliation and restoration, can be found in Jewish and Christian belief with which I was familiar, even though our houses of correction and our reformatories seldom live up to their names. The element of retribution and revenge in justice is not a primary aspect of Navaho thinking. Reflecting concretely on this, putting myself in the situation as best I can, led to questioning the assumption that justice requires making the offender suffer to balance the suffering caused by the offense. What had seemed entirely fitting in American culture came to be less obviously right. The values to be sought in justice came to be more subtle, with the satisfaction of knowing that "justice has been done" in the suffering of the moral offender now seen to be questionable as a moral value.

Concrete reflection on a practice or belief of another culture does not always result in greater appreciation of that aspect of the culture. When I reflect on the genital mutilation of girls that is practiced in some cultures, no reflection leads to admiration of the practice. Reflecting on concrete situations, no matter what role I think of for myself, male or female, young or old, does not make the practice morally appealing. My reflection is not only on the pain of the young girls, or on the lives of women who do not receive in sexual union the physical gratification most of us experience. I reflect also on the satisfaction that men must find in their position of social privilege and their power over women, including the satisfaction that they are in little danger of being cuckolded. These satisfactions are understood psychologically as I reflect on them, but they are not understood as morally valuable. The desire of both men and women to fit into a society, to accept and support the traditions of their people, can be understood, but in the circumstances these desires do not carry with them the banner of moral rectitude. I simply do not find that to understand is to accept.

Intersubjective agreement in values and moral standards is a rich source of moral insight. If we use it properly the wide range of intersubjective agreement can play an important role in judging moral claims. The wide range is necessary. Intersubjectivity must be as rich, complete, and conclusive as we can make it.

Writers on feminist ethics advocate attention to first-person narrative, the expressions of moral experience by women, oppressed people, and others not usually listened to. The concept of first-person narrative indicates a valuable way to broaden and enrich our grasp of intersubjectivity. Carol Gilligan objected to the way the moral thought and feelings of women were usually ignored; she argued that a rich source of moral insight was not becoming part of moral philosophy. In her explanation of ecological feminism, Karen J.

Warren urged listening to the voices of different people, including those who have moral backgrounds different from those with which we are most familiar.[2] Jim Cheney urges that environmental ethics be enriched with "bioregional narrative" that allows the "multiple voices of this Earth" a hearing.[3] Some of the call for listening to people's reports of their moral experience came out of the application of feminist ethics to environmental ethics, but this call for listening has relevance not only to environmental ethics, but to ethics in general. Our intersubjectivity must be intercultural.

The moral experiences of a provincial person are of far less worth than those of a person of wide intercultural experience. We are not making adequate use of intersubjectivity if we cultivate a coterie of people who will not challenge our perspectives. I once heard a schoolteacher who was described as having thirty years' experience; another person said that was incorrect— the teacher had one year of experience thirty times. If we do not seek out broader sources of intersubjectivity, we might be getting something like one person's perspectives a number of times. Just talking to a large number of people may not be adequate. We must use good judgment in evaluating what we hear. Use of intersubjectivity is not a democratic counting of votes. This is one way in which attention to personal worldviews plays an important role.

FITTINGNESS

We need not rely on intersubjectivity alone in making moral judgments. Another important tool is examining the fittingness between our values and sense of duty and the factual knowledge associated with them. The concept of moral fittingness has played a significant role in ethics, and it can assist us in the justification of moral judgments. In our reflection upon the knowledge, values, and sense of obligation which we find closely associated in our engagement with the world, we will find a definite fittingness between some of these factors that is lacking or not very strong in others.

Fittingness is such a basic aspect of our experience that it is difficult to analyze in terms of other things. It is not surprising that moral philosophers have seldom attempted to describe fittingness, but have appealed to recognition of it, counting on the reader's own experience of it. The philosopher who seems to me to have done most to clarify the nature of fittingness is Maurice Mandelbaum, who acknowledges that fittingness cannot be defined adequately, but treats it as "a phenomenally objective relational characteristic" that can be pointed out in specific experiences, a way of defining the notion ostensively. Mandelbaum says that fittingness is a relationship that can be found between an action and "the initial conditions which call forth an action." Such conditions include "past and future events which we recognize as being relevant to the choice we are to make," within a state of affairs that we believe to be realizable. An example of this is a person's having made a promise that can be kept. He describes instances of fittingness as cases of "being in harmony with," "leading to," "completing," "fulfilling," or "answering to." When keeping a promise is seen as the fitting thing to do, it is in harmony with, answering to, and fulfilling the making of the promise.[4]

The psychologist Abraham Maslow also sought to clarify the concept of fittingness, employing explanations developed in Gestalt psychology to show how certain situations require specific actions for their completion. He writes of cases in which "poor gestalten make themselves into better gestalten," as when "an incomplete series calls for a good completion." He refers to the way a "musical progression demands the right chord . . . ," and "an unfinished problem points inexorably to its proper solution." He calls the situation's demanding a specific conclusion the "dynamic" or "vectoral" quality of facts. He sees this relationship between a situation and the fitting conclusion as a bridging of the fact/value impasse.[5]

Being aware of the fittingness of a behavior or the lack of it happens more frequently than we might have realized. As a small child I heard people say that some behavior was not "appropriate." In the movies, or somewhere, I heard the colloquial version of this: "t'aint fittin'." Of course, the lack of appropriateness was in some cases just a matter of taste, which would change in time, as the attitude of many people toward women wearing shorts, or even grown men, for that matter. In other cases the realization that a behavior was not fitting was not just a matter of convention. My mother strongly disapproved of the way our neighbors in the rural community where my father was the pastor treated their servants, who were all people of color. She did not think it was appropriate to pay the cook, the maid, or the "yard man" less than they would have been paid in town. She caused considerable disturbance when she paid our helpers more than was called for by local custom. Mother's feeling of what was fitting guided her in an important moral decision. Her relationship with the nonwhite people in this small community was shaped by her awareness that it is not fitting to treat grown people as children, or to treat any person without respect, or to take unfair advantage of those without the power to defend themselves.

Apart from moral matters, we face the need for fittingness every day. One food we like does not "go with" another of our favorites, or we feel put upon if we do not have the right bread to go with a dish. A tie "goes with" one shirt, but does not look right with another. Uncle Harry's joke might have been fine at a lodge picnic, but it was not right at Aunt Jane's tea party. In a more serious situation we seek professional advice on the appropriate medicine for an illness. We all know not to go to a fine restaurant in a tee shirt, and we do not want to tip too much or too little. It can be very important to a student taking an examination to figure out what is the cube root of 551,368; the only fitting answer is 82. In trivial matters and matters of great import we try to do what is fitting and avoid doing what is not fitting.

Exception might be taken to these examples from everyday life. It might seem to miss the point of ethics if moral fittingness is no different from fittingness in respect to customs, food, clothing, mathematical series, musical progressions, and other gestalts, examples from nonmoral aspects of life that can throw light on moral matters. The examples would be beside the point (might I say not fitting?) if moral fittingness were intrinsically different from other kinds of fittingness. Is moral fittingness basically different? Maurice Mandelbaum holds that there is no distinct moral fittingness.[6]

If we cannot identify some distinctive features exclusive to and requisite for moral fittingness, Mandelbaum is correct about this. When I reflect concretely about moral fittingness, what do I find? The only basic difference I can see is that moral fittingness is found in situations that have moral significance. What I find is fittingness between a particular situation that has moral importance and an action that is appropriate in that situation. This seems to be the same as fittingness in nonmoral contexts, except for elements of the situation that are present because of the moral importance of the situation. The examples of fittingness in common experience and Maslow's examples do help illuminate the concept of moral fittingness.

Some moral philosophers might take exception to the role I am letting fittingness play in making moral judgments. Giving weight to the feeling that a behavior is morally fitting might seem to be falling into subjectivism. In defense it can be said that the concept of fittingness is not a new and uncredentialed concept. It has a respectable history in moral philosophy. I think moral fittingness might have gone out of style in a positivistic period of philosophy because no way was seen to verify a sense of fittingness. Perhaps broad intersubjective support is all we can look to. Note, however, that intersubjective verification is involved in all verification. It is exactly the sort of verification of moral insight that we would expect to find. A sense of fittingness is not to be accepted uncritically. Intersubjective verification is expected. Without the support of intersubjective agreement, a moral sense might be an interesting bit of biographical information, but even with intersubjective support it alone does not establish a moral position. Along with intersubjective support a sense of fittingness can be examined in respect to the individual worldview that spawned it. We have three tools for examining a putative moral insight. We turn next to the importance of individual worldviews and some ways we can examine them.

CRITICISM OF INDIVIDUAL WORLDVIEWS

An important tool in making moral judgments is recognition of the role played by individual worldviews in constitution of each of our lived worlds. Our worldviews influence the objects to which our attention will be directed and they influence the constitution we will place upon those objects. Moral judgments are part of this. A worldview will indicate the moral significance of a situation or an action or it will allow the situation to escape being seen in moral terms. The main reason some people are more sensitive to a moral issue than others can often be found in the different worldviews. The person who is sensitive to issues of civil liberties most likely has a different worldview from that of the person who does not see that there is a problem with the treatment of women, homosexual people, or people of color. The person who does not see why women are concerned about a matter probably has a worldview in which women are subservient to husbands and fathers. The person who does not understand why a business person refuses a deal, a "sure thing," must have a worldview in which the business person's notion of integrity has no place.

I use the term "worldview" with some trepidation, but no term is forthcoming that is not equally problematical. The term has been used in several ways, which can be confusing, but I will try to explain what I mean by a personal worldview. Some people are accustomed to using the term only for broad cultural views, such as a medieval worldview or an Enlightenment worldview. These worldviews are important, of course, and individual worldviews incorporate parts of them, even if not very systematically, but the individual personalizes these broad worldviews, relating them to the family traditions, personal values, beliefs, and other matters that make the person a distinct individual. The individual worldview is a loosely sustained combination of factors. It is a mixture of beliefs and attitudes, desires and hopes, expectations and fears, along with commitments and moral restraints, feelings of guilt, and other matters related to morality. Some of this worldview is basic and deep-seated, our way of being in the world, what Jean-Paul Sartre called the person's initial project.[8] The person's self-image is a part of this worldview, and it affects attitudes, expectations, and various aspects of the person's relationships with other people. This worldview endures to the extent that it helps define the person, helps establish the nature of the person, but it changes as the person learns, experiences success or failure, and it is influenced by other people, grows or diminishes.

Personal worldviews are dynamic as parts of them change with experiences and learning, but overall our worldviews remain fairly stable.

Ability to describe and explain an individual worldview varies from person to person. Most people speak in clichés when they try to articulate their worldviews. Often many of their beliefs are vague and have not been examined critically. The clearest beliefs may be commonplace notions and prejudices. These worldviews are important, however, for they influence the person's perception of the world and humanity. The directing of interest to certain things rather than others, attitudes and feelings about those things, judgments about matters of which the person is aware, and any sense of moral obligation are influenced by the worldview.

The person is usually unaware of the effect of the worldview; worldviews seem to work most effectively when people are not conscious of them. They operate "behind the scenes," affecting the constitution of the person's lived world. They play a large part in forming a sense of what is desirable and undesirable, fitting and unfitting, to be sought or avoided. Whether the world is constituted as a place in which domination of one racial group or one sex by another is fitting, or is constituted as a place in which injustices are problems to be corrected, is affected by basic beliefs and attitudes that are parts of an individual's worldview. If a wife is seen as arrogant and disloyal when she expresses her wishes, the roots of the judgment can be found in a worldview. If an educated, ambitious, and creative woman is seen as interesting, rather than as threatening, the source of this attitude lies in a worldview.

We ask for no special explanation when people act upon the beliefs and desires that are in their worldviews. We expect people to seek what they value and avoid what they dislike. We only wonder what caused the conduct when people act out of character. Often a person has good reason not to seek or to delay something desirable. Excessive cost, preference for something valued even more highly, or a sense of obligation to do something else can lead a person to act in an unexpected way. We are curious, however, about the reason behind uncharacteristic behavior. A friend who loves the opera might have promised to take a parent to dinner. A frequent dinner companion might be having a medical problem with wine or rich food. I go to a popular music concert instead of the ballet because I want to be with the people who are going to the concert. Such behaviors are rooted in the person's worldview. What does puzzle us is unexpected behavior that is not explained; we feel sure that there is an explanation, even one that might not be fully grasped by the one who is acting in a surprising manner. The complex of values and desires within a person's individual worldview gives rise to expectations about behavior because worldviews affect what one does.

Worldviews, unlike American citizens, are not born free and equal. Some can be seen to be in bondage to fear, some in bondage to ignorance. Some worldviews have a poor ancestry and a questionable history. Inadequate worldviews give people a mistaken view of what the world is like. They can lead a person to make mistaken judgments and to do inappropriate things. We can evaluate worldviews, however, both in respect to the ways they came to be formulated and in respect to the elements of which they are composed.

The way some worldviews are developed casts doubt on their adequacy. Without advocating what has been called scientism, an uncritical acceptance of a naturalistic metaphysics and awe of science and technology in the face of limited understanding of science, we can see that the special sciences are our best means of learning about physical and biological aspects of the world. We can see that history and the social sciences contribute most of our reliable knowledge about social matters. The person who prefers occult sources of information, such as astrology or tarot cards, to the findings of astronomy, biology, anthropology, and the other sciences is unlikely to have a sound worldview. The person who accepts the opinions of talk-show hosts and popular singers in preference to those of scholars in economics, foreign policy, child psychology, and other matters that have been carefully studied by people with high levels of education and a mastery of research methodology are probably going to have worldviews rife with prejudice and lacking in trustworthy information. It is not that the professional researchers or the experts in a field are always correct in all points, but the best refuters of mistaken experts are other experts, not people who cannot account for their opinions. My physician might not be right about the cause of my pain, but Aunt Jane is less likely to be right, and if I need a second opinion, it is best to get it from another physician.

We are not falling into an ad hominem or genetic fallacy when we criticize worldviews on the basis of their origin. It would be a logical mistake if we were using the origin as a premise in a deductive argument, but this is not what we are doing. It is one thing to point out reasons to question an opinion and another to claim to have proven that the opinion is false. Extremely biased people might say something that is true. The fortune-teller might predict a change in the stock market, while the fiscal experts' prediction fails to come to pass, but the fortune-teller's prediction is not a sound reason for choosing an investment. We are more likely to reach sound opinions through study and research than through the easier methods that many people prefer.

Criticism of worldviews on the basis of their origin is similar to a distinction made by Monroe C. Beardsley in the sorts of critical reasons employed in art criticism. One type is reasons that support a judgment of an art work by giving grounds for thinking that a work is good, such as its being created in the artist's prime, shown in major museums, and reproduced in important art history books. Another kind of critical reasons explains why the work is good, such as its masterful use of line and color, its dynamic unity, and its expressiveness. Conversely, a lack of such qualities shows why an artwork is not a fine piece of art.[8] Paul Ziff and Arnold Isenberg give similar explanations of types of critical reasons. Holding that some aspects of a worldview are faulty because they rest on nonscientific speculation about the characteristics of racial groups is like the first type of critical reasons Beardsley describes. Just as a work of art shown in a major museum might not be very good, and in fact might turn out to be a fake, an opinion about racial characteristics could be correct. It is important, however, to recognize that the works shown in the National Gallery of Art are probably going to be fine art. It is far more likely than Uncle Mike having found a masterwork at the flea market. It is more likely that the consensus of university anthropologists is correct than it is that a Nazi propagandist or a member of the militia movement has the correct opinion.

Are we limited to finding reasons related to the origins of a worldview to suspect that the view is not adequate? Can we find reasons more like the second type of critical reasons described by Beardsley? Can we find faults in a worldview that actually illustrate its inadequacy? We can find a number of such faults in worldviews.

One recognizable fault in worldviews in a significant lack of consistency. We need not become anxious about a bit of whimsy, a touch of fantasy, or even a charming bit of inconsistency in a worldview if it is in certain parts of the worldview. A worldview is enriched by elements of poetry, imagination, humor, wordplay, and acknowledged fiction. In opinions dealing with matters approached in a factual manner, however, inconsistency is a major flaw. Vagueness, or a degree of open-texturedness, are appropriate in parts of a worldview, but in those parts that we expect to approach in a matter-of-fact way, vagueness should be reduced as much as possible. There is no harm in Tim O'Hara having certain wistful feelings about the land of his ancestors and being a bit foolish about St. Patrick's Day. If Tim thinks that the Irish people are inherently better than people whose ancestors came from Senegal, this is a problem, especially if Tim feels strongly about the matter but cannot give a clear explanation of this Irish superiority.

Racial, ethnic, class, or religious prejudice are serious faults in a worldview. Not only do such prejudices stand in the way of serious research and learning, they are expressed in opinions that are not, indeed cannot be, based on sound information. Not only does such bias make people uncomfortable and threatened by sound knowledge, so that they are unlikely to find out reliable information, the opinions of a person who is seriously prejudiced are based on what the person takes to be factually certain but are the most notoriously untrustworthy sorts of opinions.

The views of a self-serving person often show the acceptance of beliefs with which the person is comfortable, the notions that the person wants to believe. The opinions that fit too well a person's monetary or political interests are rightly suspect. With some careful scrutiny, the faults in them can usually be found. They tend to be based on putative facts that do not stand up to examination. The ardent defender of unrestricted capitalism might be quite sure that nobody ever does any significant work except for monetary reward, even when the walls of the person's office are filled with plaques, framed certificates, and other objects appealing to vanity that show that people will give much time and effort for nothing more than praise and recognition.

Some worldviews are lacking in the area of values and moral commitment. The psychopathic personality is an extreme case of a lack of social concern, while some people who are able to function in a society do not really grasp the importance of the interdependencies on which a society rests. A worldview that lacks recognition of moral demands is lacking one of the most important aspects of being a human person. The proverbial person who knows the price of everything and the value of nothing does not have an adequate worldview.

Judging a person's worldview is not easy, and I might have made it sound too simple. Worldviews are not simple things, and the best of them can have some weak areas. We should not expect an individual worldview to be perfectly well-founded or adequate in all areas of knowledge. In the complex of cognitive matters, values, and volitions, there is not one pattern that we can take as the right one, the paradigm worldview. There will be disagreement among well-disposed and intelligent people about some aspects of worldviews. In respect to some things we may have to be pluralistic and agree to disagree peacefully.

As difficult as it is, however, we can recognize the difference in most cases between adequate worldviews that lead to successful and cooperative living in human societies and inadequate worldviews that lead to unnecessary conflict, harm to persons and to society itself, and ultimately to social and personal failure of the person whose worldview began badly and deteriorated after that.

SUMMARY

Our method for making moral judgments starts with concrete phenomenological reflection on our earliest constitution of the world before we have constituted aspects of the world of our primal experience as facts, as values, and as volitions. We find the elements of fact and value and of value and volition together in our most basic experience; we find this in reflection that is not greatly affected by theoretical constructions. In the context of this largely prethematic experience of the world we are not able to make final judgments about the moral sentiments that we find mingled with the elements that we will constitute as facts, so what is the value of finding no "is/ought" impasse here? It shows us that the elements of cognition, evaluation, and volition do not come to us from utterly disparate sources, as elements that we must somehow unite through logical reasoning. A relationship between what we know and what we are morally obligated to do is discovered, not created by our philosophical skill. The "is/ought" problem can be seen as originating in our assuming that we can bring together the elements needed to justify moral claims only through formal logical argument.

Finding the elements of fact together with the elements of moral obligation does not show that the moral feelings are justified, and philosophers have tried to justify them through formal logical arguments, leading us into metaethical problems and moral skepticism. In terms of formal logic there is a gap between "is" and "ought" and between fact and value. Logic is a product of a very different kind of reflection from the concrete reflection with which we began. If we do not turn to logical deduction to justify the connection we have seen between the facts of a situation and our sense of moral obligation, to what do we turn?

We have examined several tools for use in evaluating the moral elements found in concrete reflection. One tool at our disposal is intersubjective validation of our moral claims. What does intersubjective support accomplish? It shows that a moral claim is not idiosyncratic, not merely a private whim. Intersubjective support alone would not show that a claim is correct, only that it has popular support, but the wide agreement with a moral position is not insignificant. We have failed to see some of the importance of intersubjective verification of values and moral claims because we have largely limited our use of intersubjectivity to support of claims about physical aspects of the world, and when we paid attention to values and moral claims, we have attended mainly to differences of opinion and neglected the agreements.

Another tool is the recognition of fittingness between certain situations and moral actions in those situations. We are not able to define this relationship of fittingness explicitly because it is too basic to describe in terms of other things, but we experience fittingness in our daily lives. It can give significant support to moral claims, especially when joined with the other tools of judgment.

Another tool is the evaluation of individual worldviews from within which arise moral and value judgments. The soundness or inadequacy of a worldview can be recognized through examination of a number of factors. We have good reason to trust a moral claim growing out of a sound worldview and to distrust a claim dependent upon an unsound worldview, especially when the other tools of judgment confirm the evaluation based on the worldview.

What have we accomplished with our phenomenological description of moral reflection and the tools for moral judgment? We have shown that there

are resources available to us for making moral and value judgments and deciding what we should do, resources that are sadly underemployed. Even
though we have not discovered ways to make our moral and value judgments
absolutely certain, I do not take this as a failure. We have discovered what we
need to know. We should leave aside the effort to establish a foundation for
the justification of our judgments through deductive argument. What we need
to do is accept what might be inevitable limitations on moral thinking, value
judgments, and practical decisions. There is no reason why these areas of life
would be exempt from limits faced in other areas of life. We are never certain
in regard to medicine or finance. Even engineers and scientists cannot be absolutely certain. In these areas of life we have learned to go with the best
judgments, as uncertain as they may be.

Moral philosophers have generally insisted on seeking ethical systems that
can give definitive answers to every moral question, ethical approaches based
on certainty. They have insisted on seeking such systems, which is not to say
that anyone has ever found one. I fear that moral philosophers have inadvertently encouraged skepticism about morality and a subjectivistic approach to
standards of value and conduct. By scorning any system of ethics that did not
pass an impossible test of certainty, they have given the impression that moral
philosophers have not accomplished anything. They have left people with the
impression that values and morals are simply matters of personal opinion.
The profound moral insights of ages of thinkers are allowed to be passed over
for personal whim and convenience.

In a later chapter I argue that certainty in moral judgments is not necessary,
and insisting on certainty in moral philosophy has been a serious mistake.
Rather than giving us a secure system of ethics, it has led to skepticism and
subjectivism.

I have presented the advantages of engaging in concrete reflection that
does not separate the discernment of the natural aspects of objects from the
valuational and volitional aspects of our lived worlds. This mode of reflection
also has the advantage of attending to the matters themselves as they are
given, rather than turning them into abstractions and making them parts of
general intellectual models. While abstract reflection places a premium on
logical argument about abstract notions of the qualities of objects, of values,
of moral duties, and of the willing of activities, concrete reflection values the
discernment and insight that come with turning to the matters themselves.

We have discovered that moral activity need not be a matter of guessing
and hoping that the morally right thing is being done. We have discovered the
means whereby we can make sound judgments and take sound actions by using the tools for judgment, intersubjective support, fittingness, and the assessment of worldviews. We might still make some mistakes, but we will be

less likely to err than by other methods that we might use. Following tradition, listening to those who are anxious to lead us, acting according to whim and fancy, doing whatever feels good to us will not give us nearly as sound guidance as concrete reflection and reflective use of the tools for judgment and decision that we have examined.

NOTES

1. Tony Hillerman, *Sacred Clowns* (New York: Harper Paperbacks, 1993), 315–16.

2. Carol Gilligan, *In a Different Voice* (Cambridge: Harvard University Press, 1982; also Gilligan, *Mapping the Moral Domain: A Contribution of Women's Thinking to Psychological Theory and Education* (Cambridge: Harvard University Press, 1988); Karen J. Warren, "Feminism and Ecology: Making Connections," *Environmental Ethics* 9, no. 1, (spring 1987): 3; also Warren, "The Power and the Promise of Ecological Feminism," *Environmental Ethics* 12, no. 2 (summer 1990): 125.

3. Jim Cheney, "Postmodern Environmental Ethics: Ethics as Bioregional Narrative," *Environmental Ethics* 11, no. 2 (summer 1989): 117.

4. Maurice Mandelbaum, *The Phenomenology of Moral Experience* (Baltimore and London: Johns Hopkins University Press, 1969), 60–70.

5. Abraham H. Maslow, "Fusions of Facts and Values," *American Journal of Psycho-Analysis* (1963): 120, 125–29.

6. Maurice Mandelbaum, *The Phenomenology of Moral Experience*, 71.

7. Jean-Paul Sartre, *Being and Nothingness*, pt. 4, ch. 1, sec. 1.

8. Monroe C. Beardsley, "The Classification of Critical Reasons," *The Journal of Aesthetic Education*, 1968.

Chapter Four

Contextualism

Contextualism, the ethical approach that acknowledges a determinative role of the context in making actions right or wrong, helps to keep moral thinking concrete. The concrete reflection described in chapter 2 seems to me to demand a contextualist approach to moral judgment. When the context in which an action is done has a significant role in determining the moral status of the action, we are not likely to become so general and abstract in our thinking that we do not focus our attention on the factors that relevantly define our deeds and make some of them right and others wrong.[1]

WHAT IS CONTEXTUALISM?

To some extent all moral theories have had to pay some attention to the context of actions. This has sometimes been minimal, consisting only of recognizing the context in defining actions. The biblical passage most often known from the King James translation as demanding "thou shalt not kill" is given in some more recent, and more accurate, translations as "you shall not commit murder." When read this way, the need to consider the context is obvious. Murder is a legal concept. Not all acts of killing a human person are considered murder. The norms of the society and its laws must be known to define the acts forbidden in the biblical passage. Should we call the ethics based on the Bible contextual? The need to consider the context is apparent, but it would be confusing to refer to this approach as a kind of contextualism. Most supporters of the divine-command theory of ethics would acknowledge that defining an act as murder involves the social and legal context, but they would deny that any action properly called murder could ever be made morally right by the context.

Contextualism relies on the context in defining actions, but it goes further in recognizing the importance of the context. The further ways contextualism employs the context, as well as what is included in a context, will be developed as this chapter proceeds. First, let us look at another moral approach that has elements of contextualism.

Aristotle referred to contextual factors in explaining the so-called golden mean. This mean between extremes, the virtue that lay between opposing vices, was not a mathematical mean that always lay squarely in the middle between the vices. In some cases it was closer to one extreme than the other. What determined its position? To some extent the nature of the action itself did this, but also the status of the agent contributed to the placement of the mean. The courage of the soldier and the proper diet of the athlete would be foolhardy or gluttonous for the middle-aged merchant and the housewife. The nature of specific virtues could not be recognized without attention to contextual factors such as sex, age, and place in society.

Does this make Aristotle's ethics a kind of contextualism? We can see that Aristotle's understanding of justice is more contextual than is Plato's. While Plato wrote of justice as a proper balance of the three parts of the human soul, Aristotle spoke of social situations, of male householders, women, children, and slaves, but to label the moral approach of Aristotle contextualism could be more confusing than helpful. Contextualism assigns more importance to the context than did Aristotle, or it does this more explicitly.[2]

Contextualism sees the context in which a contemplated action will be performed, or in which an act was done, as an important factor in making a moral judgment. The context does more than enable a more explicit definition of the action. The moral fittingness of an action is affected by the context. Even though there are some actions that are unlikely to be morally right in any context, the moral status of many actions are dependent on the context, and theoretically any act that is usually wrong might be right in a specific situation, or a usually right action can be wrong.

Consider Mr. Brown, a farmer who is requested to grant an easement so a road can be built through his land to enable a property owner on another road, Mr. Peel, to have a closer route to his property. It would seem a good and neighborly thing for him to grant the easement, but what if he discovers that some property owners living near Mr. Peel do not want to make it profitable for Peel to bring a business into their neighborhood? Now the easement might be seen as a bad thing. Upon investigating, however, Mr. Brown discovers that Mr. Peel plans to convert his charming family home to a bed-and-breakfast inn with no more than three guest rooms. That does not seem like something that will harm the neighborhood. Mr. Brown is inclined to give the easement, but he learns that the road will need to go through a wetland area that is home to many species of wildlife that might be harmed by the road. Now the good thing has become bad again. Is this example far-fetched? Actually it is typical of the situations in which we make moral decisions, and the need to take account of one detail, then another and another, is what we should expect before we can settle on the right thing to do.

What are the contextual factors to be considered in making moral decisions in real life? One of them is the outcome, or expected outcome, of the action. One does not need to be a strict utilitarian to recognize that some actions are morally right if they result in the realization of what is valued as a good and wrong if they fail to produce good. Several different kinds of good result can be considered. Significant social benefit, improvement in personal or public health, scientific advances, or an increase in liberty or justice are grounds for approving of an action. Even when gaining some good is not sufficient by itself to make an action morally right, the securing of such goods is a right-making consideration.

The morally significant context is not limited to the consequences of the deed being judged. A number of social and legal factors must be considered. The culture of the moral actors plays an important role in moral judgment. Recognition of the importance of cultural matters does not entail accepting the ethical theory that holds that moral right and wrong are no more than cultural matters. A contextualist need not hold that moral right and wrong are relative solely to what is approved in a culture. How then do cultural matters affect moral rightness? Let us consider a simple example.

In a society in which premarital sex is frowned upon, a young woman who is persuaded to engage in a sexual relationship outside of marriage might feel that she has been misused, a judgment that would be shared by her parents and other significant people in her life. What is morally wrong in this case would be seduction, pressuring a person to do something that probably will be regretted later. The cultural context determines in part which actions will be regretted. The culture does more than help define "premarital sex." Even when we know what actions constitute premarital sex in the culture, we must consider the culture more thoroughly before we know what attitudes toward it to expect. In a culture with different mores, a woman might feel that she is not being taken seriously if a relationship does not involve sexual expression. The wrong here would be leading a person to expect what one is not intending to do. The culture determines what a person can reasonably expect.

In addition to cultural matters, factors specific to a situation affect the moral rightness of an action. We are in no position to judge whether Mary should ask the physician to discontinue the medication being given her husband, John. We need to know more about John's illness and physical and mental condition. Do the physicians consider his illness terminal? Might the medication effect a cure? Is John conscious, rational? Is he suffering greatly? What does he want? If he is not rational now, did he express a firm desire while he was rational?

The context also includes natural factors. Climate, availability of food and shelter, health, the economic system, and other factors that determine people's needs and opportunities are important considerations. This can be seen in the changed attitude of Europeans to the behavior of native peoples in Canada as reported by employees of the East India Company. What was first seen as shocking brutality, the killing of aging parents, can now be seen as acts of mercy and filial duty. The difficulty of migratory life in a harsh climate and the belief that a person spent the afterlife in the same age and health as when he or she died gives the act of killing a meaning it would not have in temperate climates in which people foresaw a life after death in which one is forever ageless.

Having to weigh many factors in making a moral judgment does complicate ethics. Later we will look at the advantages of using a contextualist approach, and I believe these will show an obvious superiority of contextualism to other systems of ethics. For now let us proceed with the observation that the cultural and natural factors are important aspects of the morality of actions. We need to reflect upon these factors when making a moral decision. Ignoring these matters would give us simplicity at the cost of making moral judgments that could be considered false and arbitrary. Our thought on them must be concrete reflection that focuses on the matters themselves before we start to apply moral principles. Treating situations as abstractions will not lead to the best moral decisions.

One difficulty to be faced is disagreement over which factors in a situation are significant morally. The contextualist is committed to making a particular judgment in the particular context, but some aspects of the situation are morally significant and some are not. How can we decide which is which? Jonathan Harrison uses the example of a sailor with a tattoo who tells a lie on a Tuesday afternoon.[3] Obviously the day of the week and the time of day are seldom matters of moral importance, although they could be significant in special circumstances. Lying, on the other hand, tends to be a wrong-making factor at all times, even when the context changes the usual significance of lying, such as when lying is necessary to prevent a terrible wrong. This is not to say that lying will be the wrong thing to do in every context, but the lying itself will never be the factor that makes the action right

It is difficult to set out simple principles for distinguishing what is morally significant in a context from those factors that do not have significance. Marcus G. Singer shows the importance of whether factors are described generically or specifically.[4] To use Harrison's sailor, "One day he told a lie" does not have the morally irrelevant aspect in "Tuesday he told a lie." This will help in some contexts, but in many cases there may be no ready substitute for good judgment.

In any case, care should be taken in the way a factor is described. What is morally significant can be missed with a deliberate or careless inadequate description. Even little children learn to describe their behavior in terms that preserve their innocence. From the child's "I was just playing" to the land developer's description of a virtually untouched parcel as "already disturbed," we can use descriptions to avoid facing the moral significance of what we do. Many of our actions have features or consequences that can be looked upon favorably or can be frowned upon. The morally important description requires being honest and being astute.

THE MORAL SIGNIFICANCE OF CONTEXTUALISM

The difference between the minimal reference to the context in ethical systems that must attend to cultural or legal factors in the definition of moral terms and the use of context in contextualism is not a trivial matter. Most ethical systems have found it necessary to acknowledge the context in some way, but most of them do not allow the context to play a critical role in the determination of moral rightness and wrongness. It is a simple matter for almost any system of morals to acknowledge the difference between "white lies" used in the interest of social harmony or to avoid hurting a person's feelings over some trivial matter and a lie told to cause a person harm. An extreme Kantian might argue that any saying of what is not true is a grievous moral wrong, but many moral philosophers would limit the condemnation of lying to the telling of a falsehood for the purpose of harming or taking advantage of a person. How does contextualism differ from this position? It would be in acknowledging that there can be situations in which telling a lie, one which would hurt someone, might be the morally right thing to do in a specific context. Denying the truth to a person bent on hurting other people would be such a situation, and causing the harm of apprehension and prosecution as a criminal to such a person might be the intended end of tricking the person into actions that would lead to arrest.

Making a moral judgment contextually can lead to acceptance of an action that would not be approved in most circumstances. The role played by the context in the decision to lie to the criminal shows that much more is involved than making the definition of a term more exact. To argue that all that attention to the context achieved was to define "justified lying, type n" to cover lying to criminals who ought to be apprehended at all costs is to stretch the description of our process of moral judgment unreasonably. We were not seeking a special definition of a moral term to make it apply to a special case. We were using the commonly accepted definition of lying and discovering that in this circumstance telling a lie was the appropriate thing to do. Only confusion and obfuscation results from giving a strained explanation of our moral thinking to bolster a favored theory or to fend off an unwelcome theory.

We do not clarify ethical theory when we make contextualism trivial by pointing out that all ethical theories must attend to the context in some way, which would make contextualism an unimportant distinction. The context is much more important for some approaches than for others. Contextualist theories allow situational factors to influence moral decisions in ways that other theories do not allow. Contextualist approaches do not turn to the situation as a regretful necessity. Rather, the context is seen as a fruitful source of information that enables moral judgment to be more complete and more adequate than abstract thinking about ethical principles would achieve. There is a significant difference between the contextualist who reflects on the moral situation in order to see more clearly the implications of the context and the moralist who treats contextual matters as annoying complications in making moral judgments.

Without weighing the importance of contextual matters, a moral judgment might be ill-fitting, even doing harm. When people decide what to do on the basis of abstract principles, the action might be one that we can see upon examination to be wrong. A responsible physician cannot know whether to tell a patient just how sick he is without knowing not only the physical condition of the person, but also the emotional state. Can we know whether to be frank with a relative about how she looks after an illness without knowing how strong she is emotionally? If these examples seem trivial, we can think of "enterprises of great pith and moment" that cannot be decided adequately just on the basis of abstract principles.

CONTRIBUTIONS OF
CONTEXTUALISM TO MORAL JUDGMENT

Contexts are necessarily specific and particular, and this keeps contextualist ethics from becoming too abstract to deal properly with the real-life decisions people must make. The moral decisions people must make are about people's needs, the possibilities present in the situation and in people's knowledge and abilities, and the possible good or harm that could result from acting in one way rather than another. This is why the person who approaches decisions abstractly is often of little help in coming to a resolution people can live with. The person who adamantly insists on principle may just as likely hold adamantly to an irrelevant principle as to one providing moral insight for the particular situation.

The contextualist approach forces attention to the details of a context. This makes less likely the overlooking of something morally significant. The focus must be on the particularities of the specific situation. This is one reason why a phenomenological approach to moral judgment has a distinct advantage over other philosophical methods. A phenomenological method requires what Edmund Husserl advocated: "returning to the matters themselves." Within concrete phenomenological reflection, the moral judgment is made in terms of the moral agent's life in the world, the world in which the moral decision will be acted upon. An abstract approach, on the other hand, leads to making the decision mainly on the basis of principles that might be far removed from the world of the agent.

Some philosophers are uncomfortable with the demand for concreteness. Philosophers have tended to find attractive the neatness and simplicity of reducing ethics to principle. There have been some unfortunate consequences of this tendency. Plato's intellectualistic ethics, finding the basis of morality in eternal and unchanging ideas, might seem to give morality a firm and unquestionable foundation. This is deceptive, however; Plato's ethics is not of much help to people who must make decisions regarding morally significant matters, since these eternal ideas are very hard to know, as Plato himself acknowledged. In one of his dialogues, he has Socrates agree that only the exceptional person can know them.[5]

Kant's abstract rule, known as the categorical imperative,[6] does not provide the sufficient material basis for moral judgments. It says nothing about important aspects of life, such as economics, sex, pain and suffering, and family responsibility, about which people must make moral decisions. There is a great deal of dispute about the role and importance of the Categorical Imperative in ethical theory. I think the most it might do is indicate a necessary condition for moral principles, a test of the validity of any putative moral principle. It does not provide us the sufficient conditions for recognizing our moral duties. The substantive content on the basis of which a moral decision can be made is not found apart from the context in which one must act.

The general principles that are commonly accepted as moral guidelines, such as the duty of nonmaleficence, the requirement that pain or harm not be inflicted upon a person gratuitously, cannot be applied without some attention to the context. Once I was treated for a dislocated shoulder by a physician who used adhesive tape, a practice not in favor with other physicians to whom I talked. The physician was peeved to discover that on the day to remove the tape I had sprayed under the tape with alcohol, so that it slipped off painlessly. People had warned me that the doctor enjoyed snatching tape off his "victims." In this context, the judgment of causing gratuitous pain seems justified. In another context, when causing the pain could not be helped, the accusation of maleficence would not be justified. The context determines whether the infliction of pain is gratuitous.

Ethics cannot be reduced to logic or to any other simple and abstract process of decision making. Ethics must deal with life and the situations in which people live. Life can quickly become more complicated and messy than the neat systems of philosophical thought. Acknowledging the importance of the context in making moral judgments may offend some philosophers, but that is a small price to pay for an approach to ethics that allows it to take all relevant matters into consideration and to guide us to decisions that will make a positive contribution to our lives.

Let us return to the uneasiness of many philosophers with a contextualist approach. There is more behind their opposition than a bias toward neatness and order. There is a fear that contextualism will lead to moral laxness, not to mention facilitating misuse of moral principles by opportunists. Some moral philosophers insist that a system of ethics must provide definitive answers to every moral question. The objections will be treated in chapter 7, which defends the adequacy of a contextual and pluralistic moral philosophy.

Why is there strong objection to acknowledging that behaviors right in one context are wrong in others? There is no logical contradiction in expecting different behavior in different contexts. An important part of our socialization is learning what is appropriate in different situations. A degree of contextualism is involved in various aspects of life. The moral aspects of life have never been free of some degree of attention to context. What bothers people about acknowledging this and applying it systematically?

For some people the reasons are theological. They have been taught that being a good person consists of obeying specific rules regardless of the outcome. Adopting a different view is too threatening for some of them to consider it. Other people might feel that a system of morality requiring thought and the careful weighing of many factors is too difficult, if not for them for the people around them. These fears of contextualism are understandable in people who have little knowledge of ethical theory or the history of philosophy. Why do philosophers hesitate before a full-fledged contextualism? I am not sure that the hesitation of philosophers is much different from that of nonphilosophers. I am not sure we should expect it to be much different. Adopting a full-blown contextualist position does involve accepting a position that has not enjoyed centuries of open philosophical acceptance. It involves a kind of risk. The value of taking the risk is not as obvious to some thinkers as it is to others.

Why should anyone take the risk of adopting an ethical approach still in the process of development? There are several reasons. One is that the approaches to morality that we learned as children were not developed to guide people through the moral dilemmas we face today. Once a philosopher told me that he had learned all he needed to know about morals from a beloved aunt. That could be a comforting thought, if one could believe it. Many of us cannot believe it. Mother, my aunts, and the ministers of religion in my youth not only did not know about the biomedical, environmental, economic, and international issues now confronting humanity, but they did not have a method of making moral decisions that is adequate to face these issues. Some of the attitudes and beliefs learned in childhood are of permanent value, but I must supplement these with an ethical method still in the making. The risk of this would not be reasonable if the newer approaches did not accomplish more than the older ones. Does attention to context help solve real-world ethical problems? Let us look at one.

The issue of human population control is difficult. Except for the defense of positions that are rooted in theology, discussion of the morality of various proposals quickly turns on contextual matters. Seeing that the problem of overpopulation is not a question simply of people in underdeveloped countries rests on recognition of the prodigal waste of natural resources in the developed countries, especially the United States, which uses a lion's share of the resources to maintain less than 10 percent of the human population. Looking at the context of this issue, we see that the American way of life, in respect to material goods, would not be possible for the world at large. Knowledge of the context shows us that even if we are able to produce enough food to feed a greatly expanded world population, a scarcity of other basic resources would be intractable. Potable water and fuel are limiting factors in providing a good life for an expanding population. Destruction of forests, desertification, and extinction of other animal and plant species would be unavoidable.

Proposals to limit human fertility can be argued on the basis of principles such as reproductive freedom, but we do not have a firm grasp of the principle when we try to understand it as an abstraction, apart from the context of problems of world population and human suffering these problems can cause. The practical issues, such as a preference for positive inducements to limit family size over some form of punishment, must face the contextual matters of differences between the situations of poorer and more affluent people. Will inducements become coercive for the poor, while allowing the wealthy freedom to reproduce as they will? We need to reflect carefully on this matter.

Even with our best thought put to the problem, population will be a critical threat to world peace and human welfare. The question of the most effective methods of reducing fertility may be solved, but there is still the problem of the large number of very young people in the population in many parts of the world, since a large percentage of people in the teens and twenties can lead to population increases even if fertility declines. We stand no chance of confronting this problem successfully if we approach it abstractly. We might not solve this problem, but we will have a better chance if we reflect concretely on the lives of young people in the context of their cultures. This may enable us to find ways to change patterns of life so that childbearing is postponed and the number of births is limited.

Employing a contextualist approach will not make the resolving of moral problems and disputes easy. It might in some case make possible a resolution that could not be reached on the basis of abstract principles alone. More often, what a contextual approach will do is bring into moral decisions factors that might otherwise be overlooked. Reflection can open our eyes to matters that abstract thought would not bring to our minds. The main argument for contextualism is that our moral decisions will have a greater chance of being correct decisions, decisions that are adequate for facing the problems of our day. This seems to be a sufficient advantage to outweigh any difficulties the approach might incur.

NOTES

1. I use "contextualism" in preference to the term "situationism," even though the latter term might be more familiar to many people; it is frequently associated with the position of Joseph Fletcher's *Moral Responsibility* (Philadelphia: The Westminster Press, 1967). Fletcher's approach acknowledges that the context must be considered in making moral judgments, but it holds that love is the one moral absolute in all situations, and I do not want my concept of contextualism to be confused with this moral approach. While I recognize love as a value, usually a right-making consideration, I am not ready to consider it an absolute or sufficient value for all judgments.

2. Aristotle *Nicomachean Ethics* 2.6; Plato *Republic* 4.435a-c, 441c-e; Plato *Phaedrus* 246a-b, 253c-254e.

3. Jonathan Harrison, "Utilitarianism, Universalization, and Our Duty to Be Just," *Proceedings of the Aristotelian Society* 1952–53), 105–34.

4. Marcus G. Singer, *Generalization in Ethics* (New York: Alfred A. Knopf, 1961), 20.

5. Plato *Parmenides* 134b–35a.

6. Immanuel Kant, *The Fundamental Principles of the Metaphysics of Ethics*, Sec. 2.

Chapter Five

Moral Pluralism

The concrete reflection that I advocate seems clearly to point to contextualism as an important part of an ethical system that facilitates the making of the most adequate moral judgments. I also believe that an adequate system of ethics will be strengthened by an acceptance of moral pluralism, but I expect more resistance to the acceptance of pluralism than to contextualism.

Traditionally philosophers have sought to found ethics on one principle, such as the principle of utility or Kant's principle of rational consistency. This would certainly make it simpler, and advocates of one position or another undoubtedly thought a monistic approach would make ethics sounder and stronger. Some moral philosophers, however, are now looking at the matter differently, seeing that a monistic approach might not make ethics stronger, but poorer. Bernard Williams holds that ethics has suffered not from too many sources of moral guidance, but from too few.[1]

The desire for enrichment of our sources of moral guidance has produced a number of recent treatments of moral pluralism. This literature deals with using multiple moral principles and multiple values, as well as different degrees to which an appeal to different sources of moral guidance is to be used.[2]

Pluralists use the moral principle that is appropriate in a given situation. When a principle or moral value is clearly applicable to the situation at hand, pluralists consider the use of the source of moral guidance justified, even if that particular principle or value has no role to play in situations of different sorts.[3]

Much of the interest in moral pluralism has been seen in environmental ethics and in feminist ethics. It is hardly surprising that environmental ethics, dealing with issues which have not been treated in ethics until recently, would be both interested in and open to new ways of approaching ethics.

Feminist ethics has an interest in pluralism because one of its thrusts is the need to make ethics more inclusive, to include insights from women and other people largely ignored in traditional ethics. Carol Gilligan's 1982 study of ways women approach moral issues supported a demand that the way women think about morality be accepted as legitimate and not be rejected because it does not agree with highly abstract and rationalistic male-dominated approaches to ethics. In the previous chapter we saw that feminist ethics often favors pluralistic approaches that make a deliberate effort to heed the voices of people who have been ignored previously; Karen Warren favors listening to first-person narratives that bring new perspectives and insights to moral philosophy, and Jim Cheney speaks of bioregional narrative in which many moral voices are heard. This openness to new voices leads to moral pluralism, as seen in descriptions of feminist ethical approaches as being like a collage and as having flexible boundaries, like a quilt.[4]

To be a responsible ethical approach, a moral pluralist theory must be able to justify using different moral principles in different situations and in making different kinds of moral judgments. This involves showing how one situation is morally different from another and why the principles used in a given situation are appropriate. It will not do to use pluralism as a way to accommodate the whims of everyone or to give a new name to the old cultural-ethical relativism. Concrete reflection must play a significant role in pluralistic ethics. It is necessary to enable the maker of a moral judgment to grasp the situation and its relevant features concretely. It can help the moral philosopher avoid using the openness of pluralism irresponsibly, for a responsible pluralism requires both understanding the kind of moral judgment being made in the given context and understanding one's personal involvement in the situation, including one's motivation.

Different writers have used the term "pluralism" in different ways. It is not helpful to use the term to refer to positions better understood as contextualism. The classic example of far northern people who shocked the English people working for the Hudson Bay Company by killing their aged relatives is not a case of pluralism. The main point in understanding the moral justification for the custom that Europeans found horrifying is the climate and living conditions, along with beliefs about the life after death. The harshness of life and the belief that after death people entered an everlasting life in their condition at the time of death led people who were acting on common principles of respect and care for aged relatives to kill them before they became terribly infirm. This example does not show that different principles were used in different cases; it shows how different beliefs and other aspects of the situation lead to actions that would be unlikely in other circumstances. Moral pluralism holds that different principles can be used in making moral decisions.

It is not necessary for the pluralist to argue that it will never be possible to unify a system of ethics around one primary principle. There is no point in making such a claim, even if the pluralist cannot foresee any way to unify morality beneficially. The point is that such unity is not needed or even desirable, and a rigorous pursuit of it might do great harm. The only unity needed is what I have referred to as structural unity; it might be called procedural or methodological unity. It is a unity of operational principles and standards developed to direct the choice of principles to be used. The choice of moral principles to use in a given situation must be justified for that situation.[5]

A unified procedure will involve understanding the situation and seeing clearly how it differs from other situations. Is it a family situation, one involving close friends or associates, or one dealing with a large number of unknown people? Are legal matters involved? What are the possibilities for good or ill, the measures needed, and the available resources? Methodological unity will require attention to what kind of moral question is at issue: a choice of personal action, judgment of a past action, the development of policy or law, or some other choice believed to have moral relevance? A responsible consideration of these matters will make morality complicated. It will not be possible to follow mechanically a simple procedure or policy, as Eugene C. Hargrove has realized.[6] The pluralist must accept the increased difficulty in making moral judgments as a price worth the advantage of making better judgments.

The books by Christopher D. Stone and Peter S. Wenz, cited previously in note 3, clearly explain the structural unity needed in responsible pluralistic ethics. They offer detailed explanations of the nature and application of pluralistic ethics.

Stone rejects monistic systems of ethics, systems that are grounded in one principle or set of logically related principles, for two main reasons. Morality involves such diverse activities as making personal choices, giving moral advice to other people, making moral judgments of past actions, deciding social policies, and judging character and attitudes. Stone uses the example of a senator who votes for legislation on the basis of utilitarian principles, but she need not be a utilitarian or even a consequentialist in personal affairs with family and friends, nor must she judge character on the basis of whether the person seeks utilitarian goals. A second problem with monistic systems is the different sorts of entities that have moral standing and the reasons for their being morally considerable. Humans are morally significant for a number of their qualities, but nonhuman animals and other morally significant entities do not have these same qualities; they must be considered morally, but for other reasons. Making one principle account for the moral considerability of all beings and entities toward which we are morally responsible would require such deforming of that principle as to make it lose its cogency.[7]

According to Stone, making every moral judgment respond to a monistic theory makes us ignore relevant data, leading us to a "bland generality" in our rules and turning our thought away from our moral convictions, so that we receive less moral direction.[8]

Stone's ethical approach is not a kind of subjectivism or ethical relativism. The choice of principles to employ in any case depends on the nature of the case. He describes morality as consisting of several "planes" or "domains," each of which enables the resolution of specific moral issues. He explains the reasons why each "domain" is different from others and how issues are settled within each. The domains differ according to whether the issue concerns persons, nonhuman animals, nations and other collectivities, or other subjects of moral consideration. He compares these planes to maps with different overlays to show different aspects of the area. The operation of these domains differs with different access to information and different relationships to the moral subjects. There cannot be the same relationship with friends, animal species, future generations, and large populations of people. The expectations, element of reciprocity, possibility of accepting risks and waiving rights, and other morally significant features will differ between the domains.[9] Stone describes how the different domains will differ in "focus," whether on individuals, larger grouping, or even ecosystems, and in "mood," whether absolute obligation, permissibility, or recognition of what would be better than alternatives.[10]

Stone does not expect a pluralistic morality to be determinate, giving a firm answer to all questions. If a system of ethics gives rules that are satisfactory in some cases but inadequate in others, and in some cases "virtually contradictory," the system need not collapse.[11] Accepting principles that are virtually contradictory from one case to another is necessary because of the complexity of our lives and the world in which we live. He makes clear in his 1988 article that he is not advocating unlimited acceptance of contradiction. If contradiction were "endemic," pluralism would have to be rejected, but occasional contradiction simply indicates an unavoidable "indeterminacy" in the system. [12]

Peter Wenz believes a pluralistic approach is needed because the traditional monistic theories fail when one of them is taken alone. A pluralistic theory can use the elements of traditional theories that are attractive in different sorts of contexts. He calls not for indiscriminate use of whatever theory one likes, but for the use of "reflective equilibrium" which modifies theories until consistency is found. Reflective equilibrium, is a way of using good judgment in making decisions on the basis of multiple principles. He holds that ethics requires use of good judgment, just as it is required in other areas of life.[13]

Wenz explains the need for different principles with a "concentric circles" approach, with circles of moral responsibility. In some circles the object of moral responsibility is close to the agent, with frequent and personal contacts, with strong and numerous obligations, while in others the agent is remote from those toward whom there is a responsibility. The closeness Wenz describes is not a matter of race or biological relationship; the circles differ with the opportunity to affect the lives of others. Duties to nonhuman animals, the biosphere, and very distant peoples will be more a matter of recognizing negative rights, compared to closer relationships in which positive rights play a larger role. Obligations to future generations and issues of property rights usually involve negative rights.[14]

Wenz does not expect a pluralistic approach to give definitive answers to all moral issues. An ethical system is adequate if it gives "unambiguous answers to some questions, . . . hedged or qualified answers to other questions, and merely indicates the kinds of matters to be considered in relation to a third group of questions."[15]

J. Baird Callicott published an article in 1990 in which he attacked moral pluralism. After reviewing some recent proposals to approach environmental ethics pluralistically, he raises some commonly held objections to pluralism, but grants that they are not serious. Pluralism might leave a person without definitive duties or even with contradictory commands, but he recognizes that pluralism has no greater problem with this than traditional systems; even Kantianism cannot avoid all conflicts of duties. There is a worry that pluralism might allow "moral promiscuity," allowing the unscrupulous to pick moral principles to justify immoral purposes, but he holds that any moral system must presuppose that moral people will use it.[16]

What Callicott sees as the real problem with pluralism becomes apparent in his claim that the ethical approaches of Paul Taylor, Holmes Rolston III, and his own ethics are not pluralistic. The difference between these approaches and those of Stone, Wenz, Hargrove, and feminists generally is that the systems he says are not pluralistic have a unified metaphysical basis. Pluralism, he says, separates ethical theory from moral philosophy. Stone's talk about different planes, he says, overlooks the fact that each different plane has a separate metaphysical background.[17]

Callicott himself advocates the use of different moral principles in different contexts. He bases protection of wild animals on their role in natural systems, which gives us the duty to avoid harming them, especially by destroying their habitat. We are not ordinarily responsible for feeding them and giving them medical care. Following the lead of Mary Midgley, he holds that we have duties to domestic animals and pets because we have made them members of a mixed community of humans and nonhuman animals. He compares different kinds of moral obligation to the growth rings in a tree, which is similar to Wenz's image of concentric circles.[18]

Why is Wenz's ethic pluralistic and Callicott's not? Callicott sees the difference not on the level of particular rules and moral principles, but on a metaphysical level. He accuses Stone, Wenz, and others of employing a different metaphysics with each different moral principle. Callicott holds that the moral criterion of Utilitarianism is based on psychological experience alone, a position reflecting the separation of the self from the world, the metaphysics of Cartesian dualism. He describes this as an atomistic and individualistic view of the human person that does not consider the interdependence of all living things. Kantianism, he says, rests on a concept of humans that stresses the possession of rationality, making it the "Enlightenment equivalent of the imago dei inhabiting all human beings" and the only important aspect of humanness. He does not think that either Utilitarianism or Kantianism is an adequate basis for contemporary ethics.[19]

Callicott sees the senator in Stone's example as acting upon positions that are incompatible. His reason seems to be that utilitarian considerations and the principles she used in personal matters and in judging character rest on different metaphysical systems.

As I see it, doing the most good for the people affected by an action does not require acceptance of the metaphysics of Bentham and Mill, nor any specific metaphysical formulation. The rightness of doing the most good is compatible with a number of metaphysical systems. Considering pain and pleasure morally relevant need not be grounded in the atomistic and individualistic philosophies of Bentham and Mill. The person who considers pain and pleasure morally relevant can look, for example, to a social sentiment theory, such as the Humean philosophy that Callicott employs. Any personalist is likely to recognize that extreme or unrewarding pain is destructive of human personality. Such Kantian concerns as consistency in behavior, keeping promises and respecting obligations, and recognizing the overridingness of moral demands do not require acceptance of Kant's concept of the human person. They can be important elements in a person's morality without the adoption of Kant's metaphysics.

Employing the moral principles often associated with Kant, along with use of moral principles supported by Utilitarians, does not mean that pluralistic moral philosophers are failing to acknowledge metaphysical baggage that they cannot really avoid carrying. Although we identify certain aspects of moral thinking as Kantian historically, they are so conceptually sound as to be necessary in any satisfactory approach to morality. Certain "utilitarian" and "Kantian" concerns are so basic that they can fit quite well within the modern metaphysical systems or worldviews that are consciously held by contemporary moral philosophers. Callicott has not demonstrated that principle-pluralism is metaphysics-pluralism in disguise.

What would a carefully developed and morally adequate pluralism be like? Stone presents two important aspects of it. Different kinds of moral judgment should apply different principles, and recognizing that an entity is morally significant, has moral standing, should be based on principles appropriate to that entity, even if the principle is not relevant to the moral standing of another entity.

Moral judgments are not all of the same kind, and moral actions encompass a wide range of activities. Deciding what one is going to do is not the same as judging a past act. Completion of an act removes a large part of the uncertainty faced while it was only contemplated. If Lynn waters Mrs. McMaster's flowers while she is out of town tending to her sick sister, Lynn wants to do good for her and hopes she will come home to a pretty yard. Flowers can be over-watered, however, so Lynn does not know for certain that twice weekly watering is doing the right thing until Mrs. McMasters drops her suitcase and says, "Wonderful! I was afraid the flowers would die." The principles behind Lynn's decision to water were probably largely utilitarian, to cause happiness and prevent the distress of seeing a yard full of dead flowers. Looking back and making a judgment of Lynn's actions would be based on approval of kindness, thoughtfulness, and a sense of responsibility.

Judging moral character is different from judging actions. Suppose the flowers did not do well because Lynn miscalculated the amount of watering they needed. The action would not be the right one, but her character might still be highly praiseworthy. Actions are judged, at least in part, on their consequences. The action that makes the flowers thrive is better than one that kills them. Lynn's character is a matter of attitudes and intentions, not of results. It is not contradictory to say that the good person Lynn did the wrong thing. The same matters are not involved in the different judgments. If we reflect on a concrete situation, such as Lynn's, we will readily understand the difference between the judgment of consequences and the judgment of character. The difference that we will see between the two will show the appropriateness of employing different principles in making the different kinds of judgments.

Moral activities such as praise and blame call for criteria not used in deciding what to do. We might refrain from praising someone who has done the right thing because the motives were wrong, which is like the principles underlying judgment of character. We might, however, refrain from praising a child who is "eating up" the praise, doing good things just for the praise. Here our concern might be the child's excessive desire to please and be praised, a character trait we do not want to encourage. Notice the difference in the two cases: in one we are concerned with what the child deserves, while in the other we are concerned about what is good for the child.

In determining laws and social policy, utilitarian concerns such as doing the greatest good have a long history of effectiveness. This does not mean, however, that we should never consider questions of justice. Our social policy needs both principles in the areas where they are appropriate. Advocacy of social actions and policies is much like the making of laws in the principles that are relevant.

Why can we not base all these judgments and activities on one principle? Such a monistic approach has been advocated, but we are familiar with criticism of utilitarianism for doing the greatest good in an unjust way. We could be more monistic in judging acts and judging character if virtues and duties were complementary, so that each duty had its virtue, each virtue its duty, but this is not the case, leaving us with praising virtue and approving of actions on the basis of different principles. One way to see the appeal of different principles in the several kinds of moral judgment and activity is that in the several cases we are evaluating different objects. Reflection should make this clear to us. Something different is being judged, and it would be stultifying to have to judge different things on the basis of just one principle. Different things are good for different reasons, and to insist that the meaning is the same in all cases requires a level of abstraction that pulls the linchpin out of rational discourse. Differences between types of judgments and actions are real differences that should make a difference.

Differences in context give us other reasons for adopting a pluralistic approach. In relations with family and our closest friends, utilitarian principles seldom guide us. Promises to people close to one, even more than promises to those more distant, can seldom be broken in order to secure a greater good. As W. D. Ross pointed out, only prevention of a very serious harm or securing of an extraordinary good can justify the breaking of a promise. This is more true when we are deciding what to do with family and friends than it is in making laws or social policy. In lawmaking promises seldom play a large role. To insist that the principles governing lawmaking and relationships with family members are the same is to turn to principles which are too formal to guide the choice of particular behaviors in common circumstances.

While in relations with family and close friends a utilitarian judgment will almost certainly be inappropriate, in social policies, that govern behavior toward people who are strangers, utilitarian principles will probably be the most sound basis. Promise keeping can play only a minor role, if any at all, when decisions are made about welfare laws. Special obligations to family members must not determine how a legislator votes on such matters. Impersonal matters usually need different principles from those that are appropriate in personal matters. The only common elements that we can identify in the various moral activities are so formal as to be unable to guide the choice of specific behaviors.

Of course, we feel a need for some sort of unity and order in our moral thinking, and we should not settle for less than we can have. A single moral principle or a set of logically related principles may never be available. A metaphysical system that would give unity to our moral thinking might not be available or might not be acceptable, for various reasons. Stone and Wenz try to unify their ethical approaches through a systematic analysis of the components of the system and the principles underlying them. Then they offer methods for the guidance of good judgment. This is a structural approach to unity, in contrast to a substantive unity. We can achieve a unified way of approaching moral issues in a systematic method for problem solving. Use of an effective method can avoid arbitrariness in moral reasoning. Understanding the structure of moral reasoning can give unity that we might not find in a set of moral principles. Pluralism need not be haphazard and disorganized. Using more than one moral principle can give us a better understanding of our principles.

Pluralism is not just using one principle at one time and another principle at another. Sometimes two principles are applicable to a moral issue. In this case, the two principles together form a more complex guide to behavior because the principles modify and limit each other. Doing the most good in a situation, finding the optimific action, that is, the action that produces the greater balance of material good over pain (a Utilitarian concept), and acting in a just manner need not be simple alternatives. We need not act entirely for justice or for human benefit. The principle of justice would prevent acceptance of an optimific situation that was clearly unjust.

At the same time, whether an act does good or harm is seen to have something to do with its being just or unjust. That most people find pleasure in an act does not insure its being just, but an act that does not do good, like an ill wind that blows nobody good, is hardly a candidate for moral endorsement. Two principles can be made to work in tandem. Of course they must not directly contradict each other by requiring incompatible actions, but they may limit each other.

How do we know which principles can be combined if no more ultimate principle shows us the way? Basically we must select those that produce behaviors that are in keeping with our basic moral insights and intuitions, those that we recognize as fitting behaviors in their contexts. Could there be some very general or formal principle on the basis of which we make the decision to combine two principles? I cannot deny that sometimes this may be possible, but I want to say three things about this. First, the burden of proof lies with those who claim that there is such a principle. Let it be produced if it can be. Second, it will accomplish little or nothing to produce a principle that is too vague or too formal to provide actual guidance in selecting or in combining specific principles for action. Third, we already have procedural principles that can give methodological unity to our decision-making process, so we are not left without recourse if no general moral principle can be realized.

That many people expect pluralism to make moral judgments difficult comes as no surprise. Deciding which consideration should determine a moral decision can be difficult in a situation in which several moral values compete, but we do not need to choose blindly between the alternative behaviors. This situation calls for careful judgment, not for whimsy. We have some time-tested criteria at our disposal, and usually they give us the guidance we need. Before we examine some of these criteria, let me make the point that there are no simple, mechanical procedures that will make it unnecessary to use good judgment.

Trying to rank the several right-making considerations does not help us very much, as Thomas Nagel has explained.[20] Even if we were able to agree on a ranking of the moral principles and values, this would not guide our judgment in some cases; in cases in which a lower-ranked principle calls for a very important action, it could take precedence over a higher-ranked principle that does not call for significant action. If achieving the best consequences for the persons involved is ranked above promise keeping, we would still have to recognize that a minor benefit to someone does not justify breaking a significant promise. Deciding that more good would result from helping in the neighborhood cleanup day would not justify breaking a promise to take your daughter to the zoo on her birthday. If the highest ranking has been assigned to keeping promises, a trivial promise might be less significant morally that someone's critical need for help. If a neighbor's house is on fire, a promise to watch the ball game on TV with another neighbor should be set aside. A very important reason to act according to a moral principle can make any ranking of principles and values insignificant.

Our decisions in cases in which principles conflict should not rest on whimsy or unexamined feelings. In most cases we can follow principles of procedure that help us decide between right-making considerations. These are not themselves moral rules, and as rules of thumb they are not absolute demands upon us. When they are not working, we must rely on our judgment in not following them, but the fact that they have been good guides in most cases should make us take care to avoid acting irresponsibly. Some of our guidelines will apply more to our efforts to accomplish a good situation, but some of them can guide our efforts to act fairly and justly.

One basis for deciding what to do is the seriousness of the situation. Preserving life is a critical consideration, of course, and avoiding great pain is important. Protection of property is not insignificant, but preserving life and avoiding pain are obviously more significant morally. We condemn the rich and powerful for actions by which they sacrifice people for the sake of property. Cost and inconvenience can be considered in some cases, but not when something more important is involved. These criteria rest on the common good judgment that reasonable people have practiced for ages. Judging the dangers people face and the extent of their pain is subject to error, but we have to do it anyway in many contexts.

The number of people who will be affected by an action is a significant consideration. It is not only pilots of airplanes who must land in the schoolyard or in a distant pasture who must be concerned with numbers. Utilitarian objectives call for making the larger number of people very happy, but fairness can also call for doing that which will give pleasure to more than a few people, especially when a number of people might deserve a reward.

In deciding what to do we need to consider how urgent the situation is. Some things that need to be done can only be done at all if done quickly. Other matters can be delayed safely. Getting a child out of the street may have a small window of opportunity, while returning the book to the library can wait for days.

Another consideration is the prospect of accomplishing the good for which we are striving. Doing good for someone is not our only moral concern, but it is an important one. The nonswimmer who jumps in the river to save a child is not a very good moral example. Visiting Uncle Peter, who is in a coma, might make Aunt Ida feel better, but it might be better to keep a promise to take your mother shopping. Certainly the giving of charity should be done with some attention to the use to be made of the gift, especially if the soliciting organization spends too much of what it receives on its own expenses. Should one consider the effect of keeping a promise? There might be situations in which this is a legitimate consideration.

The possibility of making amends can help us decide between conflicting obligations. Knowing that there will be an opportunity to make up for not keeping a promise can be an important consideration. If it turns out to be quite difficult to visit Mother on her birthday, will a longer visit in the summer make it up to her? The amount of effort one should exert to avoid a loss can depend on how permanent an injury will be. It might not only be foolish, but a moral gaffe, to climb a tree to rescue Mike's easily replaced kite.

These and other commonsense rules are not expediencies freshly created to make pluralism less threatening. Most people follow such guidelines in everyday matters, including those not usually thought of as moral problems.

They are among the practical tools of good judgment, but they can be very useful in making moral decisions. Most people have probably been using them without realizing how much guidance they provide. Unfortunately our rules of thumb do not always show us what we should do. Some moral choice will force us to act in the face of uncertainty, but this kind of uncertainty is not a special liability of pluralism. What is the connection between concrete reflection and moral pluralism? If our focus in making moral judgments is to include the particulars of the morally significant situation, the recognition that several moral principles provide insight and guidance is a relevant part of the situation. Reflection fosters not only a clear grasp of the material facts of the situation, such as who is involved; it promotes great sensitivity to the moral aspects, including the relevant principles.

Pluralism helps us take into consideration all that is morally relevant; to ignore something that is relevant does not lead to good moral decisions. Reflection helps us realize the advantages of moral pluralism by promoting a wide scanning of every situation. It leads to a healthy hesitation to act on the first available source of moral guidance. Moral monism forces the acceptance of one principle, and this can lead to the rejection of insightful principles that cannot be subsumed under the main principle. Monism does not foster the kind of careful survey of a situation and the sources of insight into the situation that is made necessary by pluralism and made possible by reflection. By its nature, moral monism pushes in the direction of abstraction and reduction, while pluralism pushes in the direction of inclusiveness, to take into account all that is morally relevant. Concrete reflection provides the wide view that shows the value of pluralism, and it becomes a valuable tool in the employment of a pluralistic approach to morals.

NOTES

1. Bernard Williams, *Ethics and the Limits of Philosophy* (Cambridge: Harvard University Press, 1985).

2. See, for example, Lawrence C. Becker, "Places for Pluralism,"*Ethics* 102 (July 1992): 707–19, 714; Michael Stocker, *Plural and Conflicting Values* (Oxford: Oxford University Press, 1990); Susan Wold, "Two Levels of Pluralism," *Ethics* 102 (July 1992): 785–98; Eugene C. Hargrove, "The Role of Rules in Ethical Decision Making," *Inquiry* 28: 3–42.

3. Andrew Brennan, *Thinking about Nature: An Investigation of Nature, Value, and Ecology* (Athens: University of Georgia Press, 1988); Christopher D. Stone, *Earth and Other Ethics: The Case for Moral Pluralism* (New York: Harper & Row, 1987); Peter S. Wenz, *Environmental Justice* (Albany: SUNY Press, 1988); Don E. Marietta Jr., "Pluralism in Environmental Ethics," *Topoi* 12 (1993): 69–80; Peter

Wenz, "Minimal, Moderate, and Extreme Moral Pluralism," *Environmental Ethics* 15 (1993): 61–74; Anthony Weston, "Comment on Callicott's Case Against Pluralism," *Environmental Ethics* 13, no. 3 (fall 1991): 283–86.

4. Carol Gilligan, *In a Different Voice* (Cambridge: Harvard University Press, 1982); Annette C. Baier, "What Do We Want in a Moral Theory?" *Nous* 19 (1985): 53–63; Karen J. Warren, "The Power and the Promise of Ecological Feminism," *Environmental Ethics* 12.2 (1990): 125–46; Eva Browning Cole and Susan Coultrap-McQuin, *Explorations in Feminist Ethics* (Bloomington: Indiana University Press, 1992); Jim Cheney, "Postmodern Environmental Ethics: Ethics as Bioregional Narrative," *Environmental Ethics* 11, no. 2: 117–34.

5. See my paper in *Topoi* and the works of Christopher D. Stone and Peter S. Wenz cited in note 3, above.

6. Hargrove, 30.

7. Stone, *Earth and Other Ethics*, 116, 118–20, 122–23.

8. Stone, *Earth and Other Ethics*, 130–31.

9. Stone, *Earth and Other Ethics*, 133–47.

10. Stone, *Earth and Other Ethics*, 156–63.

11. Stone, *Earth and Other Ethics*, 171.

12. Christopher Stone, "Moral Pluralism and the Course of Environmental Ethics," *Environmental Ethics* 10 (summer 1988): 152–53.

13. Wenz, 310, 311, 313–15.

14. Wenz, *Environmental Justice,* 310–11, 316, 317, 329–21, 324–29.

15. Wenz, *Environmental Justice,* 314.

16. J. Baird Callicott, "The Case against Moral Pluralism," *Environmental Ethics* 12.2 (summer 1990): 109–10, 110–11, 120.

17. Callicott, "The Case against Moral Pluralism," 113.

18. J. Baird Callicott, "Animal Rights and Environmental Ethics: Back Together Again," in J. Baird Callicott, *In Defense of the Land Ethic* (Albany: State University of New York Press, 1989).

19. Callicott, "The Case against Moral Pluralism," 114–15.

20. Thomas Nagel, *Mortal Questions* (Cambridge: Cambridge University Press, 1979), 128–34.

Chapter Six

The Siren Song of Certainty

The approach to morality described in the previous chapters shows a way of making moral decisions in a reasonable manner apart from the use of deductive logic, thereby avoiding the impasse that blocks arguing from factual premises to normative conclusions. Both the "is/ought" and the fact/value impasses come with the attempt to base normative judgments on formal logical arguments. Some moral philosophers will be reluctant to abandon the effort to base moral judgments on formal logical arguments because they want moral claims to have the certainty that deduction makes possible. It must be admitted that the approach I have described does not give moral claims the certainty that many moral philosophers desire and some consider necessary for an adequate ethical system.

I believe that the quest for certainty in moral philosophy has been detrimental. The appeal of certainty is not hard to understand, but I do not think certainty is necessary, and the harm it has done can be avoided. Ulysses stopped the ears of his crew with wax and tied himself to the mast in order to avoid heeding the call of the Sirens. Thus he was able to continue on his journey. I believe we will make more progress in moral philosophy if our ears are stopped to keep out the Siren song of certainty.

DOES MORAL PHILOSOPHY
WRESTLE WITH A MISTAKE?

My position is that the quest for certainty in morality has been a mistake; we would do better if we replaced a search for certainty with concrete reflection and the use of certain tools that are capable of giving us good, if not infallible, judgment. After centuries of searching, we have not found certainty in moral reasoning, but this is not cause for despair because certainty is not necessary. A system of moral reasoning that allows the basing of moral judgments on the best grounds available is adequate to guide moral choices. Such an approach can let factual information inform moral judgment and avoid subjectivism, and it is as sound and well-reasoned as judgment in other areas of life in which we are accustomed to accepting a degree of uncertainty as unavoidable.

To be modest and restrained in our moral philosophy, no longer insisting on certainty, is not to give way to an easy morality or to drop all standards. In matters of finance, health, engineering, and other important aspects of life, we recognize the difference between careful judgment and irresponsible judgments that rest on wishful thinking, whimsy, trust in unqualified advisors, superstition, and other unsound sources of guidance. To justify a judgment based on wishful thinking or the advice of a fortune-teller on the grounds that all judgments are uncertain is not wise. Some uncertain judgments are based on the soundest reasons available, while others have no sound basis. Moral judgments based on the strongest available reasons allow us to make sound and reasonable choices. Holding out for an unlikely or impossible ideal of moral reasoning does more harm than good.

In this chapter I will explain the harm that is done by a demand for certainty in moral philosophy; in the final chapter I will argue that a moral system can be responsible and sound without having certainty.

PUBLIC DISINTEREST IN ETHICAL THEORY

Thoughtful well-educated and well-read people, the people who are likely to take ethical matters seriously, often adopt a skeptical or subjectivistic approach to morals. They are frequently attracted to an ethical relativism supposedly grounded in cultural relativism. Most moral philosophers are aware of the disputes among anthropologists about the implications of differences between cultures. They realize that ethical relativism does not follow logically from cultural relativism and is probably incompatible with it. These are technical issues, however, of which most people educated in disciplines other than philosophy are not aware. It seems that apart from the philosophers, educated people adopt some form of ethical relativism, rely on religious leaders for moral guidance, or show a lack of interest in ethics as a guide to decisions about conduct.

I have been frustrated in my attempts to talk about ethics with people who are not professional philosophers. I have been led to examine two theses. The first is that most educated people, those of the sort to think about such matters at all, have adopted a superficial and shallow sort of subjectivism or an equally shallow belief that ethics is all a matter of social norms. These concepts of ethics are considered modern, sophisticated, open-minded, and in keeping with a scientific view of life. Those who reject these shallow approaches seem to be the people who, at least verbally, support an authoritarian theological approach to ethics. Seldom do I find people who have much grasp of ethics as a reasonable approach to arguable issues.

That is my first thesis, that to most educated people ethics as we philosophers do ethics is little more comprehensible than discussions of Ionic and Doric influences on Greek grammar. Many people who have no knowledge of Greek grammar believe that there is something there to be discussed if one were only interested. In regard to ethics, however, they do not seem to believe that there is anything to discuss. I believe that this thesis can be confirmed by the reader who tries to talk seriously about ethical theory with people who have received an extensive nonphilosophical education. The liberal religious leaders whose educations probably included healthy doses of philosophy have some understanding of ethical theory; I imagine they are aware of the difficulty of getting people to approach moral matters philosophically.

My second thesis is that it is not the fault of these people that they have adopted a subjectivistic approach to ethics. Moral philosophers have brought upon themselves this unfortunate situation. They have been doing this for hundreds of years. Of course, not every philosopher has contributed to this problem, and some have made strong efforts to correct the mistakes made by moral philosophy, but the general effect has been to give the public the impression that moral philosophers have nothing to teach.

Those who are involved in practical or applied ethics run constantly into this problem. The environmental ethicist, the biomedical ethicist, the business ethicist, and the legal ethicist wrestle with a public misunderstanding of what ethical philosophy is trying to do. Those moral philosophers who get involved with ethics committees, environmental groups, or community action groups find themselves in the position of having to start all over again, as though teaching a beginning course, when they try to contribute as ethicists to the discussion of a moral issue. The fact that many moral philosophers do not even have these contacts with the public says a great deal. When a group is organized to study an ethical issue, a priest, a rabbi, and a minister are among the first leaders selected. Sometimes someone who has a deeper understanding suggests adding a professor of ethics, and only after a while do the majority of group members come to see how important it is to have such a person. When I have been on panels discussing moral issues, it has been a joy to find that one of the religious leaders was knowledgeable about ethical theory. My friends and associates in environmental groups value me most for my dedication to the cause and my ability to preach to zoning committees and city councils. I really have little opportunity to talk ethical theory with them. Most of them have the same concepts of ethics that most of my students bring to class at the beginning of the term.

What are these concepts? We often hear them expressed in rhetorical questions. "Isn't it just a matter of what a person feels in his heart?" "Ethics is a private matter, right?" "Isn't it always up to the person?" "Why should anyone else tell me what to think?" This is the subjectivist side of it. At other times we hear statements indicating a naive and unexamined social relativism–ethical relativism notion of right and wrong. "After all, this is the twenty-first century" (a statement which seems to equate ethics and fashion: one wants to be up-to-date in both). "You are wrong about that, Professor. If you got out into the real world you would see what people really do" (a statement that seems to equate what is morally right with whatever people do).

THE MISTAKE

How have moral philosophers brought this on themselves? What is the mistake with which they must now wrestle? The mistake that I see was made in several related ways. One was to make ethics too abstract. Another was to make ethics a search for certainty, which made ethics a matter of knowledge, with a great deal of confusion about the kind of knowledge that is involved. The search for this knowledge often became reductionistic, since it seemed to be desirable, or even necessary, to have one systematic explanation of right and wrong.

A truly scholarly treatment of this would be exhaustive, a careful writing of much of the history of philosophy. Perhaps someday this should be done, but all I intend to do is point out certain moments in the mistaken pursuit of ethics.

Starting with abstractionism, we can see that some philosophers seemed to view abstraction as a sort of purity, of thinking and intellectual activity at its best. Notice the abstraction of Kant's categorical imperative, which mentions nothing of the ordinary life about which ethical decisions must be made. The aesthetic formalism of Roger Fry and Clive Bell pays far more attention to human feelings and pleasure than does this monument of moral philosophy. Why could aesthetic formalism be more humane than ethical formalism? Kant wanted to lay a foundation for morals that would be a priori, unaffected by human events and the facts of life. This would make it invulnerable to change and happenstance, but it also made it unresponsive to the demands of human life.

We are indebted to Kant for making us see that morality makes binding demands upon us, but these demands can be more real for us if they are seen in the context of our particular lives, not as duties of a certain kind that apply in a generic sort of way. For a more recent quest for abstraction, consider the abortive effort to create a deontic logic, which attempted to make moral demands certain by treating moral argument as analogous to modal logic. The effect of this is to base moral judgments on generalities, removing them from the particulars of daily experience. What is more purely rational, and more abstract, than a pattern for logical argument? Unfortunately, this pattern could make but a limited contribution to our resolving of moral problems.

What is wrong with this abstractionism? Several things are wrong. In the first place it was trying to achieve an absoluteness and epistemological certainty, neither of which was achieved or is needed to approach ethical decisions rationally and constructively. Another problem with making moral philosophy abstract is that moral philosophy was made an arcane discipline that most people, and not just the uneducated masses, could not relate to as a significant part of their lives. People who face ethical decisions are concerned about the human particularities within which they must live. Concrete reflection attends to these human particularities, and this is part of its value, as we saw in previous chapters. Highly abstract notions are not understood and do not seem important. Feminist ethics, with its focus on concrete aspects of life, might finally be our salvation in this respect.

Highly abstract approaches to ethics did harm in failing to succeed in doing what they were attempting. In failing to achieve an absolute and indubitable basis for moral decision, they helped convince many thinking people that ethics is not absolute and is not certain, all of which could have been a good thing, except that the connection between reason in ethics and absolutism had been so well established in people's thinking that the failure of absolutism was seen as the failure of moral philosophy.

Closely related to the turn toward abstraction was the pursuit of absolute certainty. Many paths were taken in the pursuit of certainty, and they all led the explorers astray. In some cases the certainty was based on metaphysical systems much more doubtful than the ethical duties they were supposed to undergird. In other cases the certainty was sought in epistemology, sometimes by making ethical claims a priori, which seemed, even to not-very-dogmatic empiricists, to make them analytic. One of John Locke's explanations of the nature of morality made morality true by making its ideas archetypes that are true in themselves, not by corresponding to anything in the world.[1] Locke was not the only person to talk this way, and he did have other things to say about morality, but it is not hard to see that this approach to ethics enables us to be certain at a very high cost.

The problem to be seen in Locke and others who made moral knowledge analytic, in Hutcheson and Shaftsbury and others who thought moral knowledge analogous to sense perception, and in the thinkers who held that moral knowledge is like knowledge of mathematics is that they were trying to make morality a kind of knowledge. They accounted for this in various ways, all of which tried to fit morality to an inappropriate model of knowledge. All of these attempts to make morality certain by modeling it after a familiar form of knowledge opened the way for unhelpful questions and harmful answers. We do seem to have moral insights, and we may have a moral sense, but these need to be investigated carefully with anthropological and psychological studies and their limitations made clear. We need to be careful not to make knowledge claims that will not stand up to scrutiny.

We could have listened more carefully to Aristotle, who told us that morality is a matter of practice. It requires practical, not theoretical, reasoning. It requires knowledge, but not the kind of knowledge possible in other areas of life.[2] Unfortunately, Plato's notion of morality as knowledge of ultimate truths held sway over our thinking. We had difficulty seeing that morality requires knowledge, but is not itself a kind of knowledge.

Making morality a kind of knowledge in itself, in contrast to recognizing the importance of general knowledge for moral judgment, gives rise to skepticism. Morality does not work well when seen as theoretical knowledge, but unfortunately the skepticism was turned toward morality itself, not toward the misguided theoretical formulations of morality.

BEING OUR OWN ENEMIES

Inadvertently moral philosophers fostered moral skepticism by attacks on each other in which they seemed to reject totally the insights of the philosopher criticized. They have shown the errors and inadequacies of other moral philosophers, as they should, but often have not taken equal care to show that these imperfect ethical theories made significant contributions to our understanding of the moral life. An example of this is the attacks on Philippa Foot, who challenged the belief that moral principles must be categorical. Her work was scorned as an attack upon morality.[3] What is the thinking public to assume when they see creative approaches to ethical theory condemned as an attack on morality? What can people think when monumental ethical systems are knocked down by the next generation of philosophers? The public is given the impression that ethical theory always fails.

What could have been done differently? Ethical theory could have been approached as a developing enterprise. Political theory can look upon

Athenian democracy, the Magna Carta, and other steps toward democratic government as progress toward the goal of a government that is truly of, for, and by the people. The ethical concepts of our philosophical ancestors can be seen in the same appreciative way. There is no contradiction between acknowledging the faults of old theories and recognizing that they made significant contributions.

This is part of my interest in moral pluralism. Not only did older theories contribute to the development of moral philosophy, but contemporary theories contribute to our understanding of morality, even if these are not perfect theories that will stand unchanged for centuries. Every science and every intellectual discipline, along with all of the arts, grew and improved down through the ages. Just as we honor Giotto for his pioneer efforts to bring perspective to art works, even though the perspective in his art now looks primitive to us, we can honor the philosophers who enabled us to be where we are now. Just as we honor a medical researcher for making limited progress in the cure of disease, we can recognize the contributions of moral philosophers of the past and contributions of contemporary ethical theorists.

It is up to us to make up for the mistake we made in the past. With time, we might be able to show the educated public that we are working on something significant and together are making progress.

NOTES

1. John Locke, *An Essay Concerning Human Understanding* 5, 5, 7.
2. Aristotle, *Nichomachean Ethics* 1.3.
3. See, for example, William Frankena, "The Philosopher's Attack on Morality," *Philosophy* 49 (1974): 345.

Chapter Seven

An Adequate System of Ethics

The approach to ethics explained in the preceding chapters does not attempt to deduce a set of moral principles from a metaphysical foundation or from putative intuitions of moral knowledge. It relies on concrete reflection on our moral experience, within which elements of knowledge and elements of moral demand are found together in our most original experience of our lives in the world. Since the moral aspects of this experience are not deduced from the elements of factual knowledge, there is no "is/ought" dichotomy to contend with. The moral insights realized in our reflection might be sound or unsound, so they are tested against the intersubjective experience of many people from several cultures to see that they are generally found to be fitting and are not personal idiosyncrasies. In addition, our insights must be compatible with a sound personal worldview, one that is sound both in the way it is developed and in its contents. The ethic resulting from this process is not absolute; it is contextual and pluralistic, and its demands have meaning and are binding upon us in relation to our worldviews.

The chapters on contextualism and pluralism explained why concrete reflection, as contrasted with abstract and reductive reflection, directs us toward attention to the details of the context in which a moral judgment is made and is open to many sources of moral insight. These chapters presented reasons why these approaches to ethics facilitate the making of sound ethical judgments. Some of the common objections to contextualism and pluralism were answered. In this chapter I will continue this discussion, but also I want to focus more closely on the role of the individual worldview of the moral agent, the person who must decide what is the right thing to do. The agent's worldview shapes the meaning that events have for the agent; it is within the context of the worldview that the moral obligation has significance and is felt to be binding upon the agent. The view that moral obligations are contextual has implications that many moralists have resisted. These moral philosophers have tried to make moral obligations certain and absolute. Contextual obligations are not absolute, since they are recognized in respect to particular situations, and they are seldom certain, since most situations involve elements of uncertainty. The situation in which an action is contemplated contributes part of the significance of the action, and any uncertainty about the situation adds that element of uncertainty to the moral judgment. Since the obligation is not absolute, it will not be binding upon everyone regardless of the context. When the worldview of the moral agent is recognized as part of the context, the agent is made part of the context to a degree that many moralists find unacceptable. To defend the ethical approach that I am proposing, I must deal with uncertainty and the lack of absolute moral norms.

No one has succeeded in making the case that knowledge of moral duty is certain, and I do not think anyone ever will. In fact, the goal of making morality certain is detrimental to morality, as I argue in chapter 6. What it does is to create a false and impossible notion of what morality ought to be, and this has led to unnecessary moral skepticism. When every moral theory is subjected to criticism from moralists because it does not give absolute certainty to moral knowledge, a frequent response is to take moral theories as mere opinion. Add to this the common notion that one opinion is as good as another if no opinion can be proved the true one, and a vicious subjectivism invades the concept of moral philosophy that many people hold. It is not enough, however, for me to argue that the quest for certainty cannot succeed and that the attempt has harmful consequences. It is not enough to point to the failure of attempts to justify ethical absolutism. It could be the case that a rational approach to ethics is not possible, but I do not believe this is so. What must be shown is that an ethical approach based on fittingness between a person's worldview and the person's actions, as realized in reflection on the morally relevant aspects of the person's situation, can be an adequate ethical approach.

There are some criteria for an ethical system upon which most ethicists agree. Ethics is expected to give moral demands that are binding upon the agent. The demands must not be individual tastes or self-serving desires of the agent; they must stand against a person, confront the person, and be able to override personal desires and interests. These moral demands must be universalizable, which means that they are not simply personal standards of behavior, but can be willed to be universal in application in some meaningful sense. Moral philosophers have talked about these criteria in a number of ways, but there seems to be wide basic agreement about them. There are disagreements about the interpretation of such concepts as universalizability, but most ethicists accept some version of it. I intend to show that the ethical approach I offer meets these demands adequately, even if not in the way some moral philosophers think an approach should.

I: MORAL OBLIGATION WITHOUT CERTAINTY

The notion that the context in which a moral decision is made has important bearing on that decision is not a new or radical idea. In fact, most important ethical systems have recognized the significance of the situation in some way and given it some degree of importance. Contextual matters played an important role in Aristotle's ethics and in most ethical systems since his time. Even systems of ethics based on absolute rules had to reckon with contexts in defining actions covered by the rules. Some ethical systems give more weight to the situation than others; what makes an approach to moral judgment contextual is its acknowledging that the context not only helps define the moral rule, but has significant bearing on the determination of moral obligation. I do not need to defend the general view that an ethical system can recognize the function of the context in which an action is contemplated or has been done. What I must do is explain how I see the connection between the context and the moral decision and show the adequacy and the advantages of this perspective.

One consequence of stressing the importance of context is to make the moral judgment relative to the situation, and this prevents the building of a moral system out of completely general and abstract statements. This I see as an advantage, since it forces attention to the concrete realities that are involved in the action contemplated or judged. When the context informs the moral principles, moral judgments become subject to a degree of uncertainty, and some people consider this a weakness in the ethical approach. I see it as an unavoidable aspect of ethics that deals with the realities of life; uncertainty is often a significant aspect of a specific context. It seems to me that attempts to avoid this uncertainty prevent an ethical approach from coming to grips with life, so I do not see the uncertainty of contextual ethics as a disadvantage.

Some ethicists argue that ethics cannot function without certainty about basic moral principles that apply without reference to specific contexts. The part of the context that they find especially unacceptable is the knowledge and the beliefs of moral agents, which are part of the agent's worldview. Alan Gewirth's criticism of several approaches to ethics provides an example of demands upon ethical systems that I do not believe to be necessary or even desirable. The problem that Gewirth sees with the approaches he rejects is that they fail to provide categorical obligations.[1] Contextual moral obligation as I describe it is not categorical in the sense used by Gewirth; I claim that moral obligations do not need to be categorical in this sense to be morally adequate.

Gewirth's position on this is supported by many philosophers. The widely recognized requirement that an ethical obligation be binding and universalizable might be interpreted as requiring that it be categorical in the sense that it not be dependent on context or the moral beliefs of the agent, no matter how responsibly the agent has arrived at these beliefs. In the previous chapter I mentioned that when Philippa Foot objected to this supposed necessity of ethics requiring categorical obligations and suggested instead an ethics of hypothetical imperatives, William Frankena attacked her proposal as an attack on morality.[2] Although other moral philosophers agreed with Frankena, there has been no unanimous agreement about categoricalness as a formal criterion of ethical adequacy. What is the criterion that an ethical system must meet for its obligations? Can the obligations of contextual and pluralistic ethics be binding upon the moral agent in a significantly meaningful sense, a sense adequate for a sound ethics?

When Gewirth holds that moral obligations must be categorical he means that they are "mandatory for the conduct of every person to whom they are addressed regardless of whether he wants to accept them or their results." They may not be overridden by any nonmoral requirement, such as institutional rules or laws "whose obligatoriness may itself be doubtful or variable." Categorical obligations cannot be avoided by "shifting one's inclinations, opinions, or ideals." Categorical obligations must have "certain definite contents such that the opposite contents cannot be derived from the principle that has been justified."[3] The problem I have with the standards that Gewirth lays down is the statement about the moral agent's shifting of inclinations, opinions, and ideals. He seems to think that these can be shifted at will as a person finds it convenient. He does not specify the kinds of opinions and inclinations that can be shifted easily. Some opinions are easily changed, but these are not the kind on which a responsible and intelligent person would base a moral approach. I can get tired of one of my ties and quit wearing it. I might change my opinion of a newspaper columnist on the basis of one column. These are relatively trivial matters, however, and they have no effect on my moral beliefs or behaviors. I do not think that serious personal worldviews are subject to the manipulation that Gewirth writes about.

In his work on ethics from the period after the World War I, Husserl deals with the aspects of personal identity that cannot be changed in the easy way Gewirth writes of changing opinions and inclinations. Husserl speaks of the unified self that results from the persistence of attitudes, tastes, habits, beliefs, and projects that are a "sedimentation" from our actions and the positions we have taken. This unified self-identity is undergoing development by which we change our past convictions, but this is no trivial matter. We change ourselves when we change our convictions.[4]

Of course, people can lie and attempt to justify their immorality by claiming no longer to hold a moral conviction or a belief about a situation, but actually to change a basic conviction is a change in one's nature that does not happen without the acquisition of some important new knowledge or the experience of something very important. It is not done easily as a matter of convenience. The sedimentation that Husserl speaks of sounds much like the original project of which Sartre wrote. Sartre thought that the original project can be changed, but only as a significant change in the person.[5] The beliefs and inclinations that can be manipulated with ease are not the significant part of the person's worldview that affects one's ethics.

Gewirth argues that the obligations that follow from his own system of ethics are categorical, even though his approach, which he calls the "dialectically necessary method," "proceeds from within the standpoint of the agent, including the evaluations and right-claims he makes." He thinks the agent will be logically compelled to make certain judgments; the reason for this seems to be the high level of generality with which obligations are described in what he calls the Principle of Generic Consistency. This principle, which Gewirth considers necessary from several perspectives, calls for the agent to recognize a generic right and obligation to claim freedom and well-being for the self and for others.[6]

Gewirth describes the obligations in his system of ethics as categorical, but I think his dialectical method, based on what the moral agent will accept, would make obligations far more dependent on the beliefs of the agent than he acknowledges. The obligations that he calls categorical might seem less dependent on the convictions of the moral agent, because they are more abstract and general than the ones I propose; they might not be as obviously and directly tied to the agent's worldview.

The existential connection of moral obligations with the individual worldview, even though it is not radically different from Gewirth's own approach, would keep the obligations of contextual and pluralistic ethics from meeting his test of categoricalness. The main difference between obligations in Gewirth's approach and mine is that in his approach obligations are more general and abstract than those that are found in concrete reflection on experience of life in the world. The contextual obligations that I describe meet Gewirth's tests of not being self-serving and not being matters of inclination; also they are determinate. They are, however, admittedly relative to the agent's beliefs and ideals, which are constituents of the agent's constitution of the world.

If by a categorical obligation one means a moral duty that is absolute in the sense that it is not dependent in any way on the knowledge and beliefs of moral agents, then I see no way to make the demands of contextual and pluralistic ethics categorical. If, to be categorical, the duties in question must be binding upon every rational being, and we resist the temptation to define "rational" in a question-begging way, then moral demands as I understand them are not categorical obligations.

II: BEYOND CATEGORICAL AND HYPOTHETICAL DEMAND

It is less confusing I believe to talk about the nature of moral obligation in other terms than their being categorical or hypothetical. There are better ways to understand the demandingness of moral obligations. It does not get us very far to say that a moral obligation is contingent; what makes a difference is what the obligation is contingent upon. It is easy to see that a demand that is contingent upon the agent's unexamined desires and purely private interests is not a moral demand; the demand is for a desired state of affairs, but the agent is not morally obligated to secure what is desired. Let us consider, however, a different sort of contingency; the state of affairs called for is contingent upon the agent's beliefs for its moral significance. Is not this a different matter entirely? Consider that in this latter case the state of affairs might not be one which the agent desires, only one the agent deems morally necessary.

Consider a merchant who has inherited a store from her father and mother, along with some very definite ideas about business ethics. She has had impressed on her from early childhood that a customer must be treated fairly and honestly. Goods must be of high quality and no questionable claims made for them. She feels morally obligated to practice business with the integrity with which her parents ran the family store. Is her sense of obligation categorical; is it hypothetical? Her sense of duty rests upon the beliefs she has been taught. These are beliefs that she might share with few people in the business community, but they are firmly grounded in her worldview. Does this context make her duty hypothetical? I do not think it contributes to our understanding to describe it this way. The important thing to see is that her duty is contextual and may not be binding upon all rational beings, but it is a moral imperative for her, as it was for her parents. It is binding also for anyone in her position who shares her beliefs, anyone with a worldview like hers in the relevant aspects.

What does this show us about ethical judgments? We see that they are not absolute, in the sense of not being relative to a context. They are not categorical, if by that one means that they would be binding upon every rational being, without regard to that person's worldview; at the same time, we see that no insight comes with calling these obligation hypothetical. What we find is that moral judgments are universalizable in the significant sense that the one holding them believes them binding upon all people in the same situation. This may be the only sense in which the concept of universalizability is useful. I see no value in a notion of universalizability that does not recognize all morally relevant features of a context.

Here we must make some careful distinctions. Moral judgments can be assessments of the character, virtue, integrity, etc. of the person who acts, or they can be judgments of acts themselves. One might judge an act to be right because it is in keeping with an accepted moral rule. The principle of utility, on the other hand, is a different basis for judgment of the act, asking whether it produces the greatest balance of pleasure over pain. Other moral approaches are more interested in the agent's attitude and reasons for acting. Both the teleological approach, which judges the consequences of behavior, and the deontological approach, which assesses the moral value of performing the action, have played significant roles in ethics. A complete ethical system will need elements from both approaches.

Our problem here is to determine what must be universalizable in an adequate moral system. If qualities of the agent, such as integrity, good intentions, an effort to take all relevant matters into consideration, are what can be universalized, is that enough to make the approach a moral one? If we place the weight of moral consideration on such traditional concerns as motives and character when we decide that a decision was a morally right one, we need not be claiming that the decision was the best one that could be made in terms of its consequences. Acting from moral considerations, even acting from what Kantian ethics would consider a good will, might not achieve good consequences; the right might not produce the greatest good.

To what extent should we require that the greatest good be done for an act to be considered a morally right act? It may not play any part in our moral assessment of the agent; it may play the major role in our assessment of the act itself. What I am going to suggest is that an ethical approach that recognizes the difficulty in knowing what will be the lasting good can accept this uncertainty and acknowledge that morally good people do not always agree, especially in the assessment of prospective acts in respect to their likely consequences. Such a system need not be subjectivistic; it can have fairly specific standards of ethical decision making. It can universalize certain aspects of morality.

Let us be clear about the kind of situation that will show clearly the difference between the ethical principles that I propose and other approaches. In many situations our ethical approach will be able to give definitive ethical guidance. In these situations, the choice is between something that is valued and something that is not valued, or it is between something valued highly and something valued slightly. At other times the choice is between something valuable that can be secured only now or only in one way, while the competing value can be secured later. What is valued could be an optimific state of affairs or the realization of such moral values as justice and personal integrity. In these situations, there is no significant disagreement about what the morally right action should be seeking; there is no need to be uncertain about what to do. It is only when there is no valued consequence or quality of an action that can be seen to rank above all others that the system does not provide definitive guidance. Situations do arise in which the ranking of values does not fall neatly into place; in such a situation, a rightly intentioned person will not know for certain what should be done; two well intentioned people could disagree about the best course of action to take.

First let us see that every ethical system runs into a problem at this point. Utilitarianism, even rule utilitarianism, faces this difficulty. Richard Brandt saw that the form of rule utilitarianism that he considered credible would require a "remainder rule" to handle cases in which the substantive and procedural rules did not resolve an issue. Both of his two suggested "remainder rules" had to go outside of rule utilitarianism for the principles that resolve the issue.[7]

Contemporary Kantianism has not been able to provide a rule to cover cases in which two important duties of perfect obligation call for different courses of conduct. Contextual and pluralistic ethics is probably no more vulnerable because of the lack of a formal criterion for resolving the hard cases than is any other ethical system. This is why hard cases are recognized as hard cases; they make demands upon the ethical system which the system cannot handle without employing a new, often ad hoc, stratagem. That such situations might arise is no reason to condemn the ethical system.

Life is complex and often unpredictable; an ethical system that can meet the needs of life can hardly be much more simple than life. Of course, a system of ethics that can give definitive answers to all moral questions looks very appealing at first, but then we realize the artificiality that must be necessary to make this possible. Alan Gewirth's requirement that a system always be able to give definitive answers is so strict as to be crippling. It is not a serious objection to contextual ethics to find that it works better when it does not claim an absoluteness that no other system has succeeded in justifying. It can acknowledge that it is contextual in that, first, its obligations take their meaning and their moral force from their fittingness in specific situations, and, second, a necessary part of a specific situation is the worldview of the person who constitutes that situation and must act in it.

As a result of recognizing the unavoidable uncertainty that comes with complex situations, especially unprecedented ones, a certain amount of toleration is appropriate. No matter how confident we may be of our ethical principles, we can be uncertain about the way we have seen a situation. We may not be sure that our projection of consequences of an action is correct. We may be uncertain of the relative weight to give consequences and moral values. This admission of uncertainty is not a weakness of contextual and pluralistic ethics; it is one of its strengths. We are less likely to do the wrong thing if we are honest enough not to claim more certainty than we have a right to. This is one way in which use of concrete reflection is better than appeals to intuition.

Kant is largely responsible for the emphasis on moral obligations being categorical. Kant recognized the importance of morality, and considering moral demands categorical is part of his taking it seriously. His notion of categorical obligation might not be as helpful in understanding moral judgment as a more inclusive and flexible notion of responsible judgment. Looking back at our conscientious young merchant, it seems that the part of her ethics that Kant would not accept was its dependence on the beliefs that are part of her worldview. In the second section of his book on the metaphysics of morals, Kant stressed the a priori aspects of morals. He said that the concept of duty, the ideal of moral perfection, and the supreme principles of morality are a priori. He firmly rejected the notion that basic moral ideas come from experience; what role he left for experience is still a matter of debate. It seems clear that he would not accept a very important role for an individual worldview. A worldview is largely a product of experience, not a priori; this aspect of the woman's ethics would probably keep the moral demands that she felt from being categorical for Kant. It is at this point, I believe, that Kant is not very helpful.

The obligations that the merchant felt were certainly not matters of mere prudence for her. In the face of competition from the large discount stores, her integrity might not have improved the bottom line. In what sense were these obligations hypothetical? They were hardly hypothetical for her, if by that we mean that they were obligations she should accept if she wanted such and such. These obligations were binding upon her because she believed such and such; her worldview incorporated certain realities. For her it was not a question of technical or pragmatic imperatives, such as Kant identified as hypothetical.

Because of this confusion over the terms "categorical" and "hypothetical," I suggest we drop them as we try to discover what is necessary for a position to be an ethical position. These old terms tend to confuse the issues that we need to resolve. "Categorical" is used to designate elements that include some that I agree must belong to any adequate ethics, but it also suggests a kind of absolute ethics, ruling out any contextual element. I do not think this absoluteness is necessary for moral adequacy. Kant's use of the term "categorical" inevitably influences our use of the term, and Kant used "categorical" to cover some concepts of morality which I believe to be essential and some concepts which may be too limiting. When Kant's use of "categorical" is contrasted with his use of "hypothetical," it would not seem that a categorical obligation needs to be understood as absolute and not contextual.

When Kant spoke of categorical obligations, in contrast to hypothetical obligations, he was contrasting them to obligations that are practical necessities if one is to achieve something one wants. He seemed to recognize as categorical an obligation to achieve something good in itself, rather than as a means to something desired. What he did not consider moral obligations were prudential necessities, "technical" and "pragmatic" imperatives. Kant also argued, however, that basic aspects of moral obligation are known a priori, and this gives "categorical" the connotation of being absolute.

As I understand moral obligations, they are not categorical in the sense of being known a priori and binding upon every rational creature, so I would avoid using Kant's terms. I will not call the demands of contextual and pluralistic ethics categorical, but I resist their being called hypothetical. They are not hypothetical in Kant's sense; a hypothetical imperative seems to mean for Kant something like, "If X is what is prudential for you, or necessary to secure what you want, do X." The merchant would explain herself differently. She was saying something like, "Because I believe Y, I must do X." This is not a hypothetical imperative, even if it is not independent of her worldview, not something dictated by abstract reason.

What is at stake here can be put much more clearly without using the confusing terms "categorical" and "hypothetical." A key factor is that a genuine moral imperative stands over against the agent; in one sense, the agent may not want to do what is required: a desire to do what is right may be the only reason the agent has for doing it. Obligations such as this are often referred to as overriding; they tend to override other interests and desires. This overridingness is not absolute; sometimes a competing obligation, perhaps a serious legal obligation or another moral obligation, is so strong that it cannot be overridden. Then the moral agent must leave the first duty undone. Still the bindingness of this first duty manifests itself in a strong sense of dissatisfaction, often with a feeling that something must be done to make amends. This sense of moral demand is central to understanding morality. This sense of demand and the universalizability of the demand make the obligation a moral one; we have seen that certain aspects of moral demands that are not absolute can be universalized.

I believe this analysis satisfies the legitimate concern of ethicists who hesitate to accept hypothetical imperatives into a system of ethics. Being in the context of a lived situation makes the obligation concrete; there is no abstract separation of the agent from the situation in which a choice must be made and no abstract separation of thought and feeling, of mind and body. When the meaning and importance of the situation are understood on the basis of a worldview, the agent's previous life experiences are brought into an active role again. The agent is truly engaged as a whole person in a real situation. If the role of the person's worldview is taken into account, it will be seen that the duty is not optional. If the sense of duty is supported by substantial intersubjectivity and undergirded by a responsible worldview, not only is the person's decision a moral one, it has a good chance of being the correct one.

This analysis of moral judgment has taken account of two aspects, the moral evaluation of the agent and the evaluation of the acts of the agent. The acts are evaluated in terms of moral value and in terms of their consequences. We have seen that certain qualities and behavioral patterns of the agent, such as the agent's character and way of making moral judgments, can be universalized rather simply. Integrity of motivation and intention, a sincere will to do justice and cause good to all concerned, is one side of the evaluation of the agent. The other side is the agent's use of the best available method in making a moral judgment, one that is not arbitrary and takes into consideration everything that is known to be relevant, one that follows careful reflection on the situation and the probable effects of projected actions. When we see these in a person's character and decision-making procedures, we say the person has acted morally. When we see a person adopt an arbitrary and self-serving course of conduct, we withhold our approval.

The evaluation of an act itself can be more difficult; worldviews must be examined, factual considerations must be weighed, and sometimes the needed information is not yet available. It is difficult to universalize acts themselves when we do not have enough information for making a firm judgment. At other times we do have enough information to justify our criticism of a person for making a bad judgment about a situation or about probable consequences. Since the actions of other people can affect us and the world in which we live, we cannot always withhold judgment even when we are uncertain; the fact that we may err does not justify our refraining from judgment when something important is involved. We should be as responsible as we can be, but we cannot avoid taking chances if we want to do the right thing. Only an ethical system that tries to dispense with consideration of the rightness of actions in terms of their actual consequences can avoid these difficulties.

The well-intentioned person will receive guidance from the ethical approach that I have described, and this is what we have a right to expect from ethics. There is nothing to be gained from having a system of absolute moral obligations. Behavior must be in specific contexts, and thinking about behavior is clearest when the contextual nature of obligation is recognized. Whether two contexts will be seen as sufficiently similar that the same obligations hold in both is a matter calling for judgment. The judgment will depend on a judger's constitution of the situation, and the worldview of the person constituting these situations will determine how they will be seen. This does not make the interpretation of the situation whimsical; constitution is not "seeing what you want to see," and when the importance of worldviews is recognized, these worldviews can be examined and criticized. The moral obligations that a person finds in concrete reflection upon the moral situation is genuine moral obligation when the nature of the world as constituted makes some actions fitting and others not fitting.

The relation to the context, which keeps the decision-making process in touch with life in the world, does not rob the moral obligation of its genuineness. The openness to a variety of moral principles to be used as they are appropriate adds richness to the making of moral judgments. The uncertainty that is an inevitable part of the ethical approach I have offered does not come from some fault in the ethics; it comes from the uncertainty of life itself, and the ethical approach is stronger for its willingness to acknowledge the uncertainty. This may not be an easy approach to follow, but it can give us the guidance we need in living a life of moral integrity.

NOTES

1. Alan Gewirth, "The 'Is-Ought' Problem Resolved," *Proceedings and Addresses of the American Philosophical Association* 48 (1973–1974): 36, 43.

2. Philippa Foot, "In Defence of the Hypothetical Imperative," *Philosophic Exchange* 1 (1971): 137–45; also "Morality as a System of Hypothetical Imperatives," *Philosophical Review* 81 (1972): 303–16; William K. Frankena, "The Philosopher's Attack on Morality," *Philosophy* 49 (1974): 345–56.

3. Alan Gewirth, *Reason and Morality*, (Chicago: University of Chicago Press, 1978), 1, 21.

4. Ullrich Melle, entry on "Ethics of Husserl" in *Encyclopedia of Phenomenology*, ed. Lester Embree et al. (Dordrecht: Kluwer Academic Publishers, 1997), 183.

5. Jean-Paul Sartre, *Being and Nothingness,* Part 4, chapter 1, Section 1.

6. Gewirth, *Reason and Morality*, 135, 158f, 169.

7. Richard B. Brandt, "Toward a Credible Form of Utilitarianism," in *Morality and the Language of Conduct*, ed. Hector-Neri Castaneda and George Nakhnikian (Detroit: Wayne State University Press, 1963) 133 34.

Index

About the Author

Don E. Marietta, Jr. is Professor Emeritus in Philosophy at Florida Atlantic University, having retired as Adelaide R. Snyder Distinguished Professor of Ethics and Professor of Philosophy.

He is the author of *For People and the Planet: Humanism and Holism in Environmental Ethics* (Temple University Press, 1994), *Philosophy of Sexuality* (M. E. Sharpe, Inc. Publishers, 1997), and *Introduction to Ancient Philosophy* (M. E. Sharpe, 1998. He is the co-editor, with Lester Embree, of *Environmental Philosophy and Environmental Activism* (published by Rowman and Littlefield in 1995). He has written numerous journal articles and book chapters, mostly in ethics and value theory.